WALKING ON GRAN CANARIA

About the Author

Paddy Dillon is a prolific walker and guidebook writer, with over 50 books to his name and contributions to 25 other books. He has written for several outdoor magazines and other publications and has appeared on radio and television.

Paddy has walked extensively around all the Canary Islands for this series of guides, along rugged cliff coasts, crossing deep and rocky barrancos and climbing all the highest mountains. He uses a palmtop computer to write as he walks. This makes his descriptions, written at the very point at which the reader uses them, highly accurate and easy to follow on the ground.

Paddy is an indefatigable long-distance walker who has walked all of Britain's National Trails and several major European trails. He has also walked in Nepal, Tibet and the Rocky Mountains of Canada and the US. Paddy is a member of the Outdoor Writers and Photographers Guild.

Other Cicerone guides by the author

WALKING ON GRAN CANARIA

by Paddy Dillon

CICERONE

2 POLICE SQUARE, MILNTHORPE, CUMBRIA LA7 7PY
www.cicerone.co.uk

© Paddy Dillon 2013
First edition 2013
ISBN: 978 1 85284 602 2

This book is the fourth in a new series of five guides to walking on the
Canary Islands, replacing Paddy Dillon's previous Cicerone guides:

Walking in the Canary Islands, Vol 1: West
978 1 85284 365 6
Walking in the Canary Islands, Vol 2: East
978 1 85284 368 7

Printed by KHL Printing, Singapore.

A catalogue record for this book is available from the British Library.

All photographs are by the author unless otherwise stated.

Front cover: A path short-cuts road bends between Saucillo and Hoya de Pineda,
on the way down to Santa María de Guía (Walk 11)

CONTENTS

A clear and obvious track wanders through the Barranco de la Data to Ayagaures (Walk 44)

Map Key

═══════════	major roads
───────────	walking route
───────────	extension
··············	alternative route
─ ─ ─ ─ ─ ─	long-distance (GR) route
─ ─ ─ ─ ─ ─	link
▪▪▪▪▪▪▪▪▪▪▪▪	dirt track
·············	seasonal river
───────────	river
⬭	sea/reservoir
▭▭▭▭▭▭▭▭▭▭	tunnel
⬭	town
▲	peak
▪	habitation
●	viewpoint
→	route direction
→	direction arrow
Ⓢ Ⓕ	start point/finish point
ⓈⒻ	start/finish point
ⒶⓈ ⒶⒻ	alternative start/alternative finish

Contour Key

	sea level		1000–1200m
	0–200m		1200–1400m
	200–400m		1400–1600m
	400–600m		1600–1800m
	600–800m		1800–2000m
	800–1000m	Map scale	0 0.5 1km

The Canary Islands

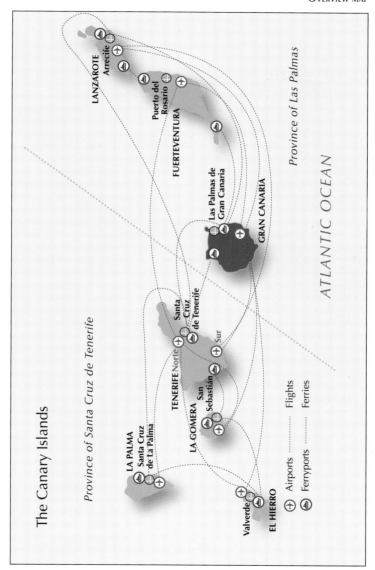

Province of Santa Cruz de Tenerife

Province of Las Palmas

ATLANTIC OCEAN

LANZAROTE
Arrecife

Puerto del Rosario

FUERTEVENTURA

Las Palmas de Gran Canaria

GRAN CANARIA

Santa Cruz de Tenerife

TENERIFE Norte

Sur

San Sebastián

LA GOMERA

LA PALMA
Santa Cruz de La Palma

Valverde

EL HIERRO

Airports ⊕ ...... Flights

Ferryports ⊖ ...... Ferries

9

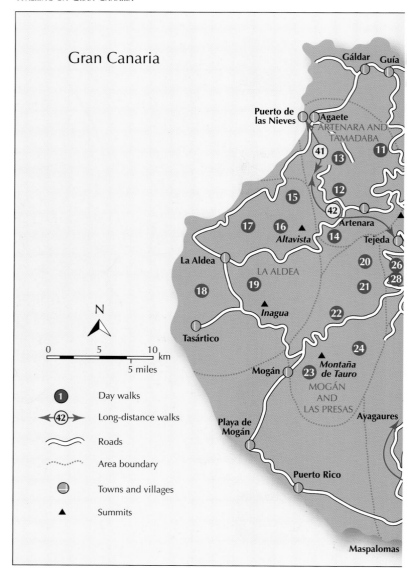

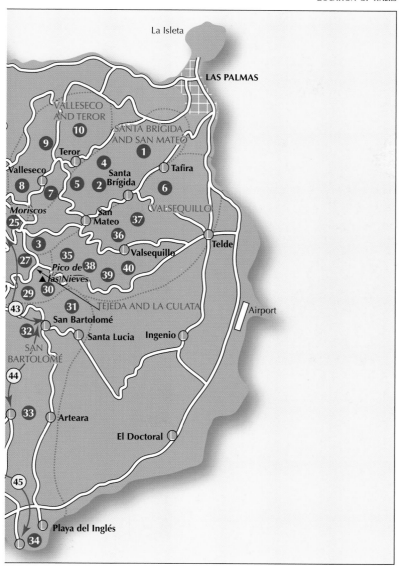

La Isleta

LAS PALMAS

VALLESECO
AND TEROR

⑩

⑨ Teror

SANTA BRÍGIDA
AND SAN MATEO

①

④ ◯ Tafira

Valleseco

⑧ ⑦ ⑤ ② Santa
Brígida

⑥

Moriscos

㉕

San
Mateo

㊲

VALSEQUILLO

③ ㉟ ㊱

◯ Valsequillo

Telde

㉗ ㊳ ㊵

Pico de
▲ *las Nieves* ㊴

㉙ ㉚

㊸ ㉛ TEJEDA AND LA CULATA

Airport

㉜ San Bartolomé

◯ Santa Lucia Ingenio ◯

SAN
BARTOLOMÉ

㊹

㉝ ◯ Arteara

El Doctoral ◯

㊺

◯ Playa del Inglés

㉞

A walker climbs towards the high gap of Degollada de Aguas Sabinas (Walk 18)

INTRODUCTION

Rugged mountains, rocky ridges and deep, steep-sided barrancos abound on Gran Canaria

The seven sub-tropical Canary Islands bask in sunny splendour off the Atlantic coast of north-west Africa. Millions of sun-starved north Europeans flock there for beach holidays, but increasingly visitors are discovering the amazing variety of landscapes throughout the archipelago. Conditions range from semi-deserts to perpetually moist *laurisilva* 'cloud forests', from rugged cliff coasts to high mountains, from fertile cultivation terraces to awesome rocky *barrancos* carved deep into multi-coloured layers of volcanic bedrock. Some areas are given the highest possible protection as national parks, but there are many more types of protected landscapes, rural parks, natural monuments and nature reserves.

More and more walkers are finding their feet, exploring the Canary Islands using centuries-old mule tracks, rugged cliff paths and forest trails. Paths pick their way between cultivation terraces, squeeze between houses and make their way to rugged coves and hidden beaches. Some paths run from village to village, following old mule tracks once used to transport goods, while other paths are based on pilgrim trails to and from remote churches and *ermitas*. Many have been cleared, repaired, signposted and waymarked in recent years, ready to be explored and enjoyed.

This guidebook explores the way-marked trail network on the large island of Gran Canaria. It includes routes of all types, from easy strolls to hands-on scrambling, from simple day walks to long-distance trails. As these routes are often fully signposted and waymarked, walkers can follow them with confidence and enjoy the island to the full. Almost 580km (360 miles) of trails are described in this guidebook.

LOCATION

The Canary Islands are more or less enclosed in a rectangular area from 13°30′W to 18°00′W and 27°30′N to 29°30′N. As a group, they stretch west to east over 450km (280 miles). Although administered by Spain, the mother country is 1100km (685 miles) away. The narrowest strait between the Canary Islands and Africa is a mere 110km (70 miles). The total land area is almost 7500km (2900 square miles), but the sea they occupy is 10 times that size.

GEOLOGY

Most of the world's volcanic land-scapes are formed where huge continental or oceanic 'plates' collide with each other. When continental plates collide, the Earth's crust crumples upwards to form mountains, and when plates are torn apart, basaltic rock from deep within the Earth's

A rocky ridge above the dirt road on the final descent towards Ayagaures (Walk 33)

mantle erupts to form mountains. The Canary Islands, however, are different, and have a complicated geological history.

The African landmass is the visible part of a continental plate that extends into the Atlantic Ocean, but the Canary Islands lie within the oceanic crust of the eastern Atlantic Ocean, close to the passive junction with the African continental plate. It is thought that the islands now lie directly above a hot-spot, or mantle plume, some 2500km (1550 miles) deep within the Earth. The mantle plume is fixed, but the oceanic and African plates are drifting very slowly eastwards. Every so often a split in the oceanic crust opens above the mantle plume, allowing molten rock to vent onto the ocean floor. As more and more material erupts, it piles higher and higher until it rises from the sea. Each of the Canary Islands was formed this way.

Lanzarote and Fuerteventura were the first Canary Islands to form, and were subsequently pulled eastwards. The next time a rift opened, the islands of Gran Canaria and Tenerife were formed, and these were in turn pulled eastwards. A further oceanic rift led to the formation of La Gomera, La Palma and El Hierro. Looking forward in geological time more islands will appear as the rift is torn open in the future.

The forces at work deep within the Earth can scarcely be imagined. Every single piece of rock throughout the Canary Islands once existed in a molten state. Consider the energy needed to melt one small stone, and multiply that to imagine the energy required to melt everything in the island chain, as well as the immense amount of rock beneath the sea that supports them all!

Over time huge amounts of volcanic material were piled high, but erosion has led to great instability. During recent geological time, vast chunks of the islands collapsed into the sea, creating features such as El Golfo on El Hierro, the Caldeira de Taburiente on La Palma, and the Orotava valley on Tenerife. With each catastrophic collapse, tidal waves devastated places around the Atlantic Ocean. Some geologists believe that the steep, bulging northern slope of El Teide could collapse during any future volcanic eruption.

WILDLIFE

Plants and flowers

While the northern hemisphere was in the grip of an Ice Age, the Canary Islands were sluiced by rainstorms, with powerful rivers carving deep, steep-sided barrancos into unstable layers of ash and lava. As the landmasses emerged from the Ice Age, the Canary Islands dried out and the vegetation had to adapt to survive. Some species are well adapted to semi-desert conditions, while on the highest parts of the islands, laurisilva are able to trap moisture from the mists and keep themselves well watered. Laurisilva forests once spread all the way round the Mediterranean and tropical regions. Small remnants of this forest survive on the higher, northern slopes of Gran Canaria, and some replanting has taken place in recent years.

Canary pines flourish on high, dry mountainsides, sometimes in places where nothing else grows. Almost every pine you see will have a scorched trunk, but they regenerate surprisingly well after forest fires. Beware of the long pine needles on the ground, as they are slippery underfoot. Canary palms also flourish in dry places, and in the past every part of the tree had a use; today they provide delicious *miel de palma*, or palm syrup. Every so often dragon trees appear, the last surviving descendants of ancient prehistoric forests. They have been decimated in the wild but prove popular in gardens.

Tagasaste trees are often found in dense plantations, always in places where livestock are grazed. They grow with little water, yet have a high nutritional content and are regularly cut for animal fodder. In recent years they have been exported to Australia. Junipers are common; fruit and nut trees have been established, including apples, oranges, lemons, bananas, almonds, figs and vines. The introduced prickly pears are abundant, not so much for their fruit, but for raising cochineal beetles, whose blood provides a vivid red dye.

White-flowered tajinaste is a bushy shrub that grows profusely in most parts of Gran Canaria

Bushy scrub is rich and varied, including sticky-leaved cistus, and a host of species that walkers should learn to identify. These include bushy, rubbery *tabaibal* and tall *cardón*, or candelabra spurge. Both have milky latex sap, as does tangled *cornical*, that creeps over the ground and drystone walls. *Aulaga* looks like a tangled mass of spines and is often found colonising old cultivation terraces in arid areas. Aromatic, pale green *incienso* is a bushy plant that, with *salado*, grows densely on many of the arid lower slopes of the islands. The fragrant Canarian lavender usually grows in arid, rocky, stony areas

Blue-flowered tajinaste, which grows only on Gran Canaria, and only in certain parts of the island

among other scrub species. Of particular importance on Gran Canaria are bushy white *tajinaste*, and the rarer blue tajinaste, which grows only on the island. Few of the plants have common English names, but all of them feature so often that they should be learned.

Flowers grow all year round, but visitors in spring and early summer will be amazed at the colour and wealth of flowering plants. Many are Canarian endemics, and even trying to compile a shortlist would be pointless. Anyone with a particular interest in flowers and other plants should carry a specific field guide, in English.

Try *Native Flora of the Canary Islands*, by Miguel Ángel Cabrera Pérez, Editorial Everest or *Wild Flowers of the Canary Islands*, by David Bramwell and Zoë Bramwell, Editorial Rueda.

Animals

As befits remote islands created in relatively recent geological time, the main animal groups to colonise the land were winged creatures, insects and birds. The largest indigenous land mammals were bats. Large and small lizards also arrived, possibly clinging to driftwood. The laurisilva cloud forest is home to the laurel pigeon, while the rock pigeon prefers cliffs. Buzzards and kestrels can be spotted hunting, and ospreys are making a slow comeback. Ravens and choughs are common in some places. There are several varieties of pipits, chaffinches, warblers and chiffchaffs. One of the smallest birds is the kinglet, a relative of the goldcrest. There are canaries, which have nothing to do with the name of the islands, and parakeets that add a flash of colour. The islands attract plenty of passage migrants, as well as escapees from aviaries. The coastal fringes are colonised by gulls, but it is best to take a boat trip to spot shearwaters or storm petrels, as they spend most of their time on open water. Boat trips are also the way to spot a variety of dolphins and whales.

Once the Guanche people arrived and colonised the islands over two thousand years ago, the forests

17

Heritage features abound, such as this fine windmill near Mógan (Walk 23)

suffered as much from clearance as from grazing by voracious sheep and goats. Following the Conquest in the 15th century, the Spanish brought in other domestic animals; of these the cats had a particularly devastating impact on the native wildlife, practically wiping out giant Canarian lizards, which have only recently been rescued from the edge of extinction. The largest lizards on Gran Canaria survived near Las Palmas simply because they were adopted as pets! Rabbits chew their way through the vegetation and appear regularly on Canarian menus.

NATIONAL PARKS

The Canary Islands include a handful of national parks and many other protected areas. There is no national park on Gran Canaria, but large parts of the island have been protected in other ways, such as Parque Rural (Rural Park), Parque Natural (Natural Park), Paisaje Protegido (Protected Land), Reserva Natural Especial (Special Nature Reserve), Monumento Natural (Natural Monument), and so on. Prominent notices usually tell walkers when they are entering or leaving these areas. There are visitor centres where more information can be studied, and where interesting literature is on sale.

THE FORTUNATE ISLES

Myths and legends speak of 'The Fortunate Isles', or 'Isles of the Blessed', lying somewhere in the Atlantic, enjoying a wonderful climate, bearing all manner of fruit. Sertorius planned to retire there, while Plutarch referred to them many times, though Pliny warned 'these islands, however, are greatly annoyed by the putrefying bodies of monsters, which are constantly thrown up by the sea'. Maybe these scribes knew of the Canary Islands, or maybe they were drawing on older Phoenician or Carthaginian references. Some would even claim that the islands were the last remnants of Atlantis.

The Gaunches, often described as a 'stone age' civilisation, settled on the Canary Islands well over 2000 years ago, and Cro-Magnon Man was there as early as 3000BC. No-one knows where the Guanches came from, but it seems likely that they arrived from North Africa in fleets of canoes. Although technologically primitive, their society was well-ordered, and they had a special regard for monumental rock-forms in the mountains.

The Guanches fiercely resisted the well-armed Spaniards during the 14th century Conquest of the islands, but one by one each island fell. Tenerife capitulated last of all, with the mighty volcano of El Teide grumbling throughout. Many Guanches were slaughtered or enslaved, but some entered into treaties, converted to Christianity and inter-married. They lost their land and freedom, but their blood flows in the veins of native Canarios.

Gran Canaria – famous for decades with people who just wanted to take things easy!

The Canary Islands were visited by Christopher Columbus on his voyage of discovery in 1492. Subsequently, they were used as stepping stones to the Americas, with many Canarios emigrating. The Canary Islands were exposed and not always defended with military might. They were subject to pirate raids, endured disputes with the Portuguese, were attacked by the British, and suffered wavering economic fortunes.

There was constant rivalry between Tenerife and Gran Canaria, with the entire island group being governed from Las Palmas de Gran Canaria from 1808, before Santa Cruz de Tenerife became the capital in 1822. In 1927 the Canary Islands were divided into two provinces – Las Palmas and Santa Cruz de Tenerife.

In the early 20th century, the military governor of the Canary Islands was General Franco, who launched a military coup from Tenerife. This led to the creation of the Spanish Republic, marking the onset of the infamous Civil War, and a long dictatorship. The Canary Islands remained free of the worst strife of the Civil War, but also became something of a backwater. It was largely as a result of Franco's later policies that the Canary Islands were developed from the 1960s as a major destination for northern Europeans.

Since 1982 the islands have been an autonomous region and there have been calls for complete independence from Spain. The islanders regard themselves as 'Canarios' first and 'Spanish' second, though they are also fiercely loyal to their own particular islands, towns and villages.

GETTING THERE

There are plenty of options for flying direct to Gran Canaria, scheduled and charter, from many British and European airports. The hardest part is checking all the 'deals' to find an airport, operator, schedules and prices that suit. Both international and domestic flights operate from the airport on Gran Canaria.

Frequent, fast and cheap Global buses link the airport with the city of Las Palmas and the southern resort of Maspalomas, and the taxi fare is reasonable. Two ferry companies link Gran Canaria with neighbouring Tenerife (via Puerto de las Nieves) and Fuerteventura (via Las Palmas) – Lineas Fred Olsen and Naviera Armas.

WHEN TO GO

Most people visit the Canary Islands in summer, but it is usually too hot for walking. Winter weather is often good, but on Gran Canaria, expect some cloud cover and rain on the mid-slopes and highest parts. Spring weather is sunny and clear, while the vegetation is fresh and features an amazing wealth of flowers. Autumn weather is often good, but the vegetation often seems rather scorched after the summer.

ACCOMMODATION

Most visitors to the Canary Islands opt for a package deal, so they are tied to a single accommodation base in a

Colour-banded waymark posts indicate paths through the Dunas de Maspalomas (Walk 34)

A walker follows a fine stone-paved path down from Pargana to Cruz Grande, passing cliffs (Walk 43)

faceless resort. This is far from ideal and a base in the 'wrong' place can make it difficult to get to and from walking routes. Out-of-season, walkers would have no problem turning up unannounced on the doorsteps of hotels and pensións and securing accommodation. It's also possible to take short self-catering lets with ease. Simply obtain an up-to-date accommodation list from a tourist information office as soon as you reach the island.

Opportunities to camp are abundant, with 20 basic state-run campsites available, often in remote and scenic locations. Although the campsites are entirely free of charge, permits have to be applied for in advance and collected in person before travelling to a campsite. See the notes at the end of Appendix C for an explanation of how to obtain permits and locate the campsites. Wild camping is technically illegal, but is also surprisingly popular.

HEALTH AND SAFETY

There are no nasty diseases on the Canary Islands, or at least, nothing you couldn't contract at home. Water on Gran Canaria is either drawn from rainfall, impounded in reservoirs or generated by a steady drip-feed from forests, where it soaks into the ground, is filtered through thick beds of volcanic ash, and emerges pure and clean, perfectly safe to drink. Natural water supplies are augmented by desalinated water, which is perfectly safe to drink, but some people don't

like the taste. Bottled water is available if you prefer, but buy it cheaply from supermarkets, rather than at considerable expense from bars. There are no snakes, no stinging insects worse than honey bees, and there are always warning signs near hives. Don't annoy dogs and they won't annoy you. Dogs that are likely to bite are nearly always tethered, so keep away.

In case of a medical emergency, dial 112 for an ambulance. In case of a non-emergency, all islands have hospitals, health centres (*centro de salud*) and chemists (*farmacia*). If treatment is required, EU citizens should present their European Health Insurance Card, which may help to offset some costs.

FOOD AND DRINK

Every town and most of the villages throughout the Canary Islands have bars. Most bars also double as cafés or restaurants, often serving tapas, which are often in glass cabinets, so you can point to the ones you want to eat. Shops are often available, selling local and imported foodstuffs. Always make the effort to sample local fare, which is often interesting and very tasty. The availability of refreshments is mentioned on every walking trail, but bear in mind that opening hours are variable. Some shops take a very long lunch break, and not all businesses are open every day of the week. Some shops are closed all weekend, or at least half of Saturday and all of Sunday.

LANGUAGE

Castilian Spanish is spoken throughout the Canary Islands, though in most resorts and large hotels, there are English and German speakers. Those who travel to remote rural parts will need at least a few basic phrases of Spanish. Anyone with any proficiency in Spanish will quickly realise that the Canarios have their own accent and colloquialisms. For instance, the letter 's' often vanishes from the middle or end of words, to be replaced by a gentle 'h', or even a completely soundless gap. Listen very carefully to distinguish between La Palma (the island) and Las Palmas (the city). The latter becomes 'Lah Palmah'. A bus is referred to as an *autobus* in Spain, but as a *guagua* throughout the Canary Islands. Some natives may sieze the opportunity to practice their English with you, while others may be puzzled by your accent. No matter how bad you think you sound, you will not be the worst they've heard!

MONEY

The Euro is the currency of the Canary Islands. Large denomination Euro notes are difficult to use for small purchases, so avoid the €500 and €200 notes altogether, and avoid the €100 notes if you can. The rest are fine: €50, €20, €10 and €5. Coins come in €2 and €1. Small denomination coins come in values of 50c, 20c, 10c, 5c, 2c and 1c. Banks and ATMs are mentioned where they occur, if cash is needed. Many accommodation providers accept major credit and debit cards, as will large supermarkets, but small bars, shops and cafés deal only in cash.

COMMUNICATIONS

All the towns and some of the villages have post offices (*Correos*) and public telephones. Opening times for large post offices are usually 0830–1430 Monday to Friday, 0930–1300 Saturday, closed on Sunday. Small post offices have more limited opening times. Mobile phone coverage is usually good in towns and villages, but can be completely absent elsewhere, depending on the nature of the terrain. High mountains and deep barrancos block signals. Internet access is sometimes offered by hotels so, if relying on it, please check when making a booking.

WALKING ON
GRAN CANARIA

*A clear path descends scrub-covered slopes
from the Casas de Tirma to El Risco (Walk 17)*

INTRODUCTION

*The upstanding Roque Bentayga was sacred to
the original Guanche inhabitants of Gran Canaria (Walk 20)*

Situated in the middle of the archipelago and one of the larger Canary Islands, Gran Canaria is often referred to as a miniature continent due to its variety. Its fringes are heavily eroded, scored by dozens of steep-sided rocky barrancos and, as a result, walks that lead in and out of them are often very rugged. By contrast, the highest parts of the island, although very rocky and riven by more deep, steep-sided barrancos, also feature gentler slopes in many places. Pine forests completely encircle the mountains, while some moist northern parts feature laurisilva 'cloud forest'. Access to the coast is good in some places, but in other places is limited to the mouths of the barrancos, due to sheer cliffs on either side.

The big city of Las Palmas is the largest settlement in the Canary Islands, and naturally it offers the fullest range of services and facilities, including abundant hotel accommodation. The most popular tourist resorts are Maspalomas and Playa del Inglés, which lie beside each other on the south coast. There are plenty of small towns and villages around Gran Canaria. Some cater for tourists and are small resorts in their own right, while other places see tourists come and go and the services on offer are distinctly Canarian.

The southern, eastern, northern and central parts of Gran Canaria are very well settled, with small towns and villages, farming hamlets and individual farms and houses climbing higher and higher up terraced and forested slopes. By contrast, the western part of the island seems arid and scorched, with fewer settlements. The large overall number of settlements, and ever-present steep slopes, ensures an incredibly convoluted road network that appears quite confusing on maps. Hidden from sight, however, are the remains of ancient mule paths that once linked many places. Many of these have been cleared, repaired, signposted and waymarked to create the core of a trail network. There are plans to expand this in future, particularly with the addition of long-distance walking trails, so keep an eye on developments. Walkers following the long-distance GR 131 trail from island to island may be disappointed to learn that the route wasn't signposted at the time of writing, but much of its planned course is followed towards the end of this book.

The central part of Gran Canaria boasts several mountains rising well above 1000m, while the highest point on the island is Pico de las Nieves, where the 1949m (6394ft) summit is out-of-bounds and enclosed as a military site. As the name suggests, it can snow at that height, although very rarely. It is worth bearing in mind that low cloud can completely obscure the mountain-tops, and in those conditions it is well to choose lower routes, which are abundant. In case of rain,

Las Palmas de Gran Canaria – the biggest city in the Canary Islands, with a splendid sandy beach

Despite the mountainous terrain, a network of well-constructed paths link all the settlements (Walks 29 and 31)

it is best to follow village-to-village routes, as there will often be handy bars offering shelter, and bus services if an early finish is needed.

It takes time to explore Gran Canaria properly, and some walkers return year after year, revisiting well-known walks and looking for completely new ones. The routes in this guidebook are arranged a few at a time in tightly-defined areas, but there are often abundant links between one route and adjacent routes, allowing plenty of room for walkers to adapt and amend each route. In any case, the convoluted road system makes it difficult to dash all over the island, so a more leisurely approach is recommended.

The 45 days of walking on Gran Canaria are made up of 40 one-day walks, many of which are signposted as PR (*pequeño recorrido*), or shorter SL (*sendero local*) routes. A five-day long-distance trail offered at the end of the book is based largely around what should become a signposted GR (*gran recorrido*) route in the future. This final trail intersects with over a quarter of the one-day walks in the book, so again there is plenty of scope to adapt and amend the route if desired. There are almost 580km (360 miles) of trails described in this guidebook, and this represents only part of the signposted and waymarked trail network.

GETTING THERE

By air
Most visitors fly direct to Gran Canaria from the UK or mainland Europe, using a variety of airlines. Local flights

from the adjacent Canary Islands are operated by Binter Canarias, tel 902-391392, www.bintercanarias.com. Frequent, fast and cheap Global buses link the airport with the city of Las Palmas and the resorts of Maspalomas and Playa del Inglés. Taxis are also available at the airport.

By ferry

Two ferry companies operate between Gran Canaria and the neighbouring islands of Tenerife and Fuerteventura. Lineas Fred Olsen, tel 902-100107, www.fredolsen.es, is quick and expensive. Naviera Armas, tel 902-456500, www.naviera-armas.com, is slower and cheaper. Sailings to and from Tenerife operate from Puerto de las Nieves, which is regularly served by bus from Las Palmas. Sailings to

and from Fuerteventura operate from Las Palmas and the ferryport is within walking distance of the city centre.

GETTING AROUND

By bus

Many years ago Gran Canaria was served by two bus companies – Salcai in the south and Utinsa in the north. They merged as Global, tel 902-381110, www.globalsu.es, but services still reflect the old north/south divide. The network is excellent, but two timetables are needed – north and south – and both must be consulted in places where separate services meet. Given the complexity of Gran Canaria's road network, and the number of settlements rising from the

Road access is sometimes exceedingly long, slow and convoluted, especially this road above Mógan

coast to the mountains, buses seem to run in all directions and often vary their routes, so timetables need careful study. Obtain up-to-date timetables for the whole island as soon as possible, from the Global website, bus stations at Las Palmas or tourist information offices. Tickets are for single journeys and fares are paid on boarding the bus. Tickets valid throughout the island are no longer available, and the only bargain tickets are for set routes, of little use to visitors and walkers. Buses are referred to as *guaguas*, although bus stops, or *paradas*, may be marked as 'bus'.

By taxi

Long taxi rides are expensive, but short journeys are worth considering. Taxi ranks are located throughout Las Palmas and in the huge resort of Maspalomas, as well as in many small towns and villages around Gran Canaria. Fares are fixed by the municipalities and can be inspected on demand, although negotiation might be possible.

Car hire

Some people will automatically pick up a hire car in Gran Canaria, and this is easily arranged in advance or on arrival. In some instances, a car is useful to reach a walk in a remote location, and using a car might sometimes offer more flexibility than using bus services. However, some of the best walks on Gran Canaria are linear, and

if you park a car at one end it can be very difficult to return to it.

Planning your transport

To make the most of walking opportunities, and limit long and awkward travelling, it is best to choose a number of accommodation bases with good bus connections. Linear routes described in this book generally start at the higher end and finish at the lower end, but there are exceptions. Where buses serve both ends, timetable details need to be checked, and you need to pace yourself to fit in with the schedules. In the few places where bus services are extremely limited, or completely absent, the only options are to arrange drop-offs and pick-ups, either by taxi or by arrangement with a car-driving friend. Pick-ups require careful planning and timing so as not to inconvenience or alarm those who are waiting for you.

WHAT TO TAKE

If planning to use one or two bases to explore, then a simple day pack is all you need, containing items you would normally take for a day walk. Waterproofs can be lightweight and might not even be used. Footwear is a personal preference, but wear what you would normally wear for steep, rocky, stony slopes, remembering that hot feet are more likely to be a problem than wet feet. Lightweight, light-coloured clothing is best in bright sunshine, along with a sun hat and frequent applications of sunscreen.

If planning to backpack around the island, bear in mind that there are several very basic camp grounds, but permits have to be negotiated in order to use them, and this can be confusing and time-consuming for a visitor, as it requires negotiations with municipal authorities, and the collection of paperwork. Wild camping is technically illegal, although surprisingly popular. Lightweight kit should be carried, as a heavy pack is a cruel burden on steep slopes in hot weather. Water can be difficult to find, so try and anticipate your needs and carry enough to last until you reach a village, houses or bar where you can obtain a refill.

WAYMARKING AND ACCESS

Gran Canaria only recently adopted a system for signposting and waymarking routes using standard European codes. The island has a network of short PR (pequeño recorrido) routes, which are marked with yellow and white paint flashes, and numbered to keep them separate. Signposts will read 'PR GC…', with a number following the letters (apart from those in La Aldea, which at the time of writing have yet to be designated numbers, and are currently given as 'PR GC XXX'). These codes are quoted in the route descriptions so that walkers will always be able to check that they are going the right way. There are also GR (gran recorrido) routes planned, but these weren't available

Many paths have been designated 'PR GC' on Gran Canaria

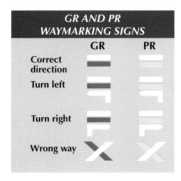

GR AND PR WAYMARKING SIGNS

	GR	PR
Correct direction		
Turn left		
Turn right		
Wrong way		

on Gran Canaria at the time of writing. They are intended as long-distance walks, but can also serve as simple one-day linear walks. Some short links are marked as SL (sendero local), literally 'local walk'.

Apart from signposts, routes are marked by occasional paint marks, parallel yellow and white stripes for the PR routes, with red and white stripes for the GR routes, and green and white stripes for the SL routes. These confirm that walkers are still on course, and usually appear at junctions. Left and right turns are indicated with right-angled flashes, but if the paint marks form an 'X', this indicates that a wrong turn has been made.

MAPS

The Instituto Geográfico Nacional (IGN), www.cnig.es, publishes maps of the Canary Islands at scales of 1:50,000 and 1:25,000. These are part of the Mapa Topográfico Nacional (MTN) series. To avoid disappointment, please check the style and quality of these maps before making a purchase, since they generally don't show the sort of details that walkers require.

One of the more built-up cave houses at Acusa Seca (Walk 14)

Rugged slopes rise on all sides from the bottom of the Caldera de Bandama (Walk 6)

On Gran Canaria, the best general map of the whole island is the 1:50,000 Kompass map of Gran Canaria, available in the United Kingdom with an Automobile Association cover, as the AA Island Series 7 – Gran Canaria. The evolving trail network does not yet feature on maps, although routes are often outlined on map boards around the island, from which details can be copied and transferred to other maps. Some of the municipalities have produced leaflet maps covering some trails, notably around Valsendero and Valsequillo, and it is worth enquiring locally for these.

Maps can be ordered in advance from British suppliers such as: Stanfords (12–14 Long Acre, London, WC2E 9BR, tel 0207 8361321, www.stanfords.co.uk), The Map Shop (15 High Street, Upton-upon-Severn, WR8 0HJ, tel 01684 593146, www.themapshop.co.uk) or Cordee (tel 01455 611185, www.cordee.co.uk).

The sketch maps in this guidebook are at a scale of 1:50,000 and all maps are aligned with north at the top of the page.

FOOD AND DRINK

Gran Canaria is self-sufficient in terms of fruit, vegetables and fish. While some restaurants are cosmopolitan, others offer good local fare. Specialities include goats' cheese. Wrinkly potatoes (*papas arrugadas*) cooked in salt are surprisingly refreshing in hot weather, served with hot *mojo roja* sauce and gentler *mojo verde*. The most popular fish dishes are based on *vieja*. If any dishes such as soups or stews need thickening, reach for the roasted flour *gofio*, which also serves as a breakfast cereal. Local wines are also available. Never pass an opportunity to indulge in local fare!

TOURIST INFORMATION OFFICES

There are nearly 30 tourist information offices spread around Gran Canaria, including a handful in the city of Las Palmas and a handful in the twin resorts of Maspalomas and Playa del Inglés. The rest are spread around several small towns and villages throughout the island, and are listed in Appendix C. The main tourism website for Gran Canaria is www.grancanaria.com.

EMERGENCIES

The pan-European emergency telephone number 112 is used to call for assistance throughout the Canary Islands, linking with the police, fire or ambulance service, for a response on land or at sea. The Guardia Civil telephone number is 062, and it is likely they would be involved in a response involving mountain rescue, as they generally patrol rural areas.

USING THIS GUIDE

The walks are spread around the island and where they lie side-by-side links between routes are often possible. Day walks are described first near the city of Las Palmas, stretching from village to village towards the high mountains. Afterwards, routes are explored in the northern part of the island, then the western part, working towards the central high mountains. The southern and eastern parts of the island are explored last, with some routes then linking with the first routes described in the book. Finally, a long-distance route is described, taking five days to cross Gran Canaria from coast to coast, via the central mountains. This will one day largely be signposted as the GR 131 trail. This route can of course be followed as a series of linear one-day walks broken at intervals.

On arrival on Gran Canaria, visit a tourist information office as soon as possible and ask for an accommodation list, and any information about walking opportunities that they stock. Remember to pick up leaflets about any visitor attractions that seem interesting, as they usually give full contact details, opening times and admission charges. Visit a bus station or bus information kiosk for up-to-date bus timetables. After that, you should have all the information you need to enjoy the walks to the maximum.

SANTA BRÍGIDA AND SAN MATEO

The Barranco de la Mina, near Utiaca. Despite steep slopes, this area is very well-settled (Walk 5)

Walkers based in the big city of Las Palmas might imagine that they are cut off from good walking opportunities around Gran Canaria, but there are plenty of bus services running early until late to nearby villages, giving access to a surprising range of rural walks. The very long and deep Barranco de Guiniguada can be entered from the old city centre at Vegueta, then followed for one, two or three days, linking villages while rising gradually towards the mountains in the centre of the island, where the paths are much steeper.

There are fine walks from village to village, suitable for walkers who prefer to sample rural scenery and small farms, while having ready access to bars and restaurants for food and drink. The walks from Santa Brígida and San Mateo to Teror are short pilgrim trails, leading to the basilica of Nuestra Señora del Pino. Most of the walks in this section are linear, and with excellent bus services there is no need to retrace steps and no need for a car. The most outstanding volcanic landform near Las Palmas is the Pico de Bandama and Caldera de Bandama, offering a splendid half-day walk.

WALK 1
Las Palmas to Santa Brígida

Start	Vegueta, Las Palmas
Finish	Santa Brígida
Distance	16km (10 miles)
Total Ascent	550m (1805ft)
Total Descent	50m (165ft)
Time	5hrs
Terrain	Easy roads and tracks, with occasional rugged paths, rising through a valley.
Refreshments	Plenty of choice in Las Palmas. Bars near Jardín Canario. Shop at Las Meleguinas. Bars in Santa Brígida.
Transport	Regular daily buses link Santa Brígida and Las Palmas, serving Jardín Canario and Las Meleguinas.

Vegueta is the oldest part of the big, bustling city of Las Palmas, and the Cathedral is its most notable building. Surprisingly, there is rapid access from the city into the Barranco de Guiniguada. Either walk all the way to Santa Brígida, or just walk halfway and explore the exotic Jardín Canario.

Route uses PR GC 02.

Most traffic avoids **Vegueta** and hurtles along the coastal Avenida de Canarias, while a busy dual carriageway, the Autovia del Centro, heads inland. Follow the quiet Calle de Juan de Quesada inland, running parallel and left of the main road, rising gently past the original university building. Cross a **footbridge** spanning half the dual carriageway, then go through a tunnel beneath the other half. Climb steps to Calle Álamo and turn left. ◄ Follow the quiet road onwards as it descends and narrows, becoming a track into the **Barranco de Guiniguada**.

Down to the left, beside the dual carriageway, is a signpost for the PR GC 02.

Turn right to follow the track gently up the bed of the barranco, which is flanked by masses of tangled scrub (dominated by bushy white tajinaste), but also supports banana plantations and palms. Always stay in the bed

of the barranco, avoiding other tracks climbing from it. The steep slopes are sometimes terraced, sometimes buttressed with concrete, with quarries and caves in a couple of places. Sprawling suburbs rise above the cliffs-tops.

Eventually, pass beneath a slender dual carriageway **bridge** on towering concrete supports. Further along, leave the track to follow a rugged, narrow path in the pebbly, bouldery bed of the barranco, squeezing past scrub at

Entering the Barranco de Guiniguada, on the outskirts of Vegueta, Las Palmas

LAS PALMAS
Lomo Apolinario
Cathedral
Footbridge
Vegueta
Barranco de Guiniguada Walk 1
San Juan
Lomo de la Cruz
Bridge
Lomo Blanco
University

Map continues on page 38

This is worth a visit. Climb steps to explore 'El Túnel' – a narrow tunnel ending with a 'window' overlooking the barranco.

Map continues on page 40

Free entry from 0900 to 1800 daily.

times. When another track is joined, the recreational site of **Fuente Morales** lies off-route to the left. ◄

Turn right along the track, Camino del Maipez, reaching a signposted junction beside some pines. The PR GC 02 runs straight ahead along another narrow and pebbly path, squeezing through cane thickets and tajinastes bushes. Follow another track onwards, which rises from the barranco and passes a few houses, overlooking another steep-sided barranco. Keep left at a junction, then the track later drifts right. A small **bridge** is reached where a busy road crosses, beside the Bar Restaurante Maipez, over 200m (655ft). Walk straight ahead up the road, with a decorative fence alongside. A pleasant garden can be explored here, but further along, just past the Bar Cafeteria Flor Canaria, is the **Jardín Canario**. ◄

Jardín Canario

Walkers with a particular interest in botany could happily spend the rest of the day here. The paths in the barranco and on the steep cliffs beyond are worth exploring, using a free map from the exhibition centre. Steep flights of stone steps lead to the top-most viewpoint, then come down by a different route and find the longest way back to the entrance. Highlights include small areas of laurisilva, dragon trees, pines, palms, cacti, a small waterfall and lily ponds. An incredible number of Canarian species are represented, as well as species from Madeira, the Azores, Mediterranean and other parts of the world.

Continue up the busy road, later turning quickly right and left as signposted for El Cañón. When the road climbs

steeply, turn left along a track to the bed of the **Barranco de Guiniguada**. Turn right up the bed, under a derelict foot-bridge supported by a stone column. The path is narrow and pebbly, flanked by grass, with steep scrubby slopes either side. Go under a narrow bridge and pass a few houses, sometimes walking on concrete, but mostly on pebbles. There are floodlights up to the left, and a path zigzags up to the village of **La Calzada** if an exit is needed.

The broad, pebbly bed of the barranco features masses of tabaibal and is flanked by cliffs. A number of slender aqueducts span the barranco, as well as a grace-ful arched road **bridge**. The rugged path reaches tree-shaded picnic tables near a *lavadero* (communal washing place), where things become easier. A track leads away, reaching a junction beside an electricity pylon. Turn right and stay on the clearest track through a broad area dotted with fields, farms and houses. Pass a picnic site shaded

A path through a small wetland in the lower part of the interesting Jardín Canario

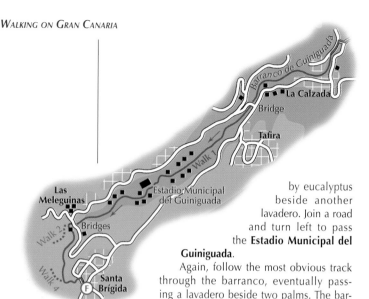

by eucalyptus beside another lavadero. Join a road and turn left to pass the **Estadio Municipal del Guiniguada**.

Again, follow the most obvious track through the barranco, eventually passing a lavadero beside two palms. The barranco narrows and there are two road bridges ahead, at **Las Meleguinas**, over 400m (1310ft). ◄ To continue onwards, walk under the bridge on the left to find a three-way signpost. Back is for Las Palmas, left is for Santa Brígida and right is for Las Lagunetas (Walk 2).

An early finish is possible before the bridges, climbing steps to a road, where buses can be caught to Santa Brígida or Las Palmas. There is a shop nearby too.

Turn left and the path narrows, going through a tunnel beneath a house. The barranco is flanked by tall walls, while terraces above bear oranges. Follow the path to a junction where the Camino Pa'l Pino (Walk 4) is signposted to the right. Turn left instead up a winding, stone-paved and then concrete path. Walk up Calle Muro into **Santa Brígida** and turn right along Calle Real to a busy road junction, over 500m (1640ft) (shops, bars, post office, banks with ATMs, buses and taxis). ◄

Walk 37 also finishes here.

WALK 2
Las Meleguinas to Las Lagunetas

Start	Las Meleguinas
Finish	Las Lagunetas
Distance	14km (8½ miles)
Total Ascent	850m (2790ft)
Total Descent	50m (165ft)
Time	5hrs
Terrain	A rugged barranco walk with occasional narrow paths, then a good track, mostly gently uphill, but steep at times.
Refreshments	Shop at Las Meleguinas. Bars at Utiaca and Las Lagunetas.
Transport	Regular daily buses from Las Palmas and Santa Brígida to Las Meleguinas. Occasional buses from Utiaca to San Mateo, Santa Brígida and Teror. Occasional buses from Las Lagunetas to San Mateo, Cruz de Tejeda and Maspalomas.

The walk up through the barranco from Las Meleguinas is quite difficult in places, but later a fine track rises gently and easily to Utiaca. Careful route finding is needed further upstream on steep slopes, then a clear track climbs from the barranco to a road network at Las Lagunetas.

Start at the shop at **Las Meleguinas**, around 400m (1310ft). Take the Pino Santo road, but almost immediately turn right under a road bridge. Turn right again under another road bridge and walk towards a three-way signpost for the PR GC 02. Left is for Santa Brígida (Walk 1), so keep right and a narrow path quickly expires in the bouldery bed of the **Barranco Alonso**. Some parts of the bed are impassable, so watch carefully for paths running parallel on the right or left. Rampant vegetation includes tangled scrub and trees. Apart from a good stretch of path along a concrete pipeline, the bed is rugged all the way to a road bridge near **Los Silos**. ▶

Route uses PR GC 02.

Walk 4 crosses this bridge.

*A road bridge
spans the Barranco
Alonso near the little
settlement of Los Silos*

The rugged, bouldery bed gives way to a path passing an information board. Watch out for more paths, either trodden through scrub, or along concrete terraces, in preference to the streambed. Sometimes there are rocky cliffs alongside. ▶ Eventually, a few houses cling to the slopes of the **Barranco de la Mina**, and a good path is followed. This becomes a track keeping left of a white building, but it peters out afterwards.

Watch carefully to spot more paths, particularly those avoiding dense thickets of cane in the streambed. Rows of houses stand on the brow of the barranco at **La Solana**. Look out for the large entrance to **Pozo La Umbria** on the left, and follow a track winding uphill from it. Turn right along a level terrace path and then go down a track back into the Barranco de la Mina.

The track is easy and rises gently past a few little buildings and cultivation plots among the scrub and cane thickets. There are increasing numbers of buildings and almond trees (Walk 5 crosses the barranco) as the track becomes concrete and climbs to a road and signpost. Turn right down the road towards **Utiaca**, where the Bar Restaurante Guiniguada is located, below 800m (2625ft). There are bus stops and a large lavadero.

A signpost points up a track for Las Lagunetas. Cross the barranco bed beside another lavadero and follow the track uphill, now concrete and climbing steeply. When the track suddenly

Look up to spot a fine dragon tree.

Map continues
on page 44

swings left,
keep straight ahead
along a grassy path, then
drop into the barranco with
the aid of a rope. Cross the stream and
scramble awkwardly up the other side, then find a

43

A clear track rises gently through the Barranco de la Mina to a road and bar at Utiaca

way back across the stream to link with a nearby concrete path.

Follow the path uphill, broadening as it passes buildings, later crossing the stream to reach a junction with a concrete road at **Ariñez**. Turn sharp left to follow the road back across the stream. Concrete gives way to tarmac on the way up through woods, reaching a turning space. Go down a concrete road, crossing the stream, then follow the road up to its end. Climb a short, steep concrete path and turn left in front of a little **house**.

Walk along a narrow terrace, watching carefully for the path on a steep slope of tangled scrub. Little paint blobs help with route-finding on the way to a

44

water catchment building and a **bridge**. Cross the bridge and climb steeply up a bendy track on the **Ladera de las Habas**. Houses are reached at the top, and the route continues up the most obvious bendy roads through the village of **Las Lagunetas**.

Eventually, pass a junction where there is a wayside shrine not far from a church, which lies above the road. Go straight past a road junction to reach a roundabout and bus stops. Follow the road onwards and gently downhill, eventually reaching a bus shelter where the road crosses the barranco. A signpost points uphill, where Walk 3 begins.

WALK 3
Las Lagunetas and Cruz de Tejeda

Start/Finish	Las Lagunetas
Distance	8km (5 miles)
Total Ascent/Descent	550m (1805ft)
Time	3hrs
Terrain	Steep and narrow paths, tracks and roads on both forested and cultivated slopes.
Refreshments	Bars at Cruz de Tejeda. Bar at Las Lagunetas.
Transport	Occasional daily buses serve Las Lagunetas and Cruz de Tejeda from San Mateo, Tejeda and Maspalomas.

This circular, or triangular, route has three elements. First is a steep climb through a well-vegetated barranco. Next is an easy walk along a forested crest to Cruz de Tejeda. Finally, the descent links a variety of paths, tracks and roads to return to Las Lagunetas, where aniseed-flavoured bread is a speciality.

Start at **Las Lagunetas**, where there is a bus shelter between two large signs for the Barranco de la Mina. A signpost for the PR GC 02 points up a track into the barranco. Follow the track past a few houses and continue up

Route uses PR GC 02 and PR GC 40.

45

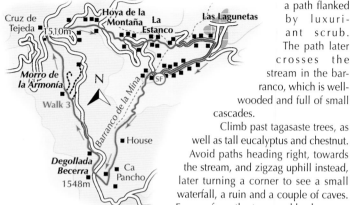

a path flanked by luxuriant scrub. The path later crosses the stream in the barranco, which is well-wooded and full of small cascades.

Climb past tagasaste trees, as well as tall eucalyptus and chestnut. Avoid paths heading right, towards the stream, and zigzag uphill instead, later turning a corner to see a small waterfall, a ruin and a couple of caves. Emerge from the trees and bushes near a house and walk up a grassy slope bearing bouldery terraces. The streambed is dry on a slope of broom and later it is flanked by stone walls.

Crossing a streambed in the Barranco de la Mina, above the village of Las Lagunetas

When a building, **Ca Pancho**, is seen to the right, follow its access track up to a road on **Degollada Becerra**, at 1548m (5079ft). This is the end of the PR GC 02, and

a signpost points back to Las Palmas. A fine viewpoint across the road takes in Roque El Fraile, Roque Nublo, Roque Bentayga, Altavista, and distant El Teide on Tenerife. A path leads to a nearby visitor centre that might well be closed. ▸

Walk 27 starts here and Walk 43 passes.

Turn right to follow the road, which is also the PR GC 40, in the direction of Cruz de Tejeda, but soon switch to a fine stone-paved path running parallel. This rises and falls gently, passing a building. Follow the road up through a pine forest, emerging from the trees where there is a view down to Las Lagunetas and the Barranco de la Mina. To the left are a stone-paved ramp and a gritty path across a slope of volcanic ash. This links with a track, which rises among pines on the slopes of **Morro de la Armonía**.

Pass a building in a fenced enclosure around 1600m (5250ft) and follow a path onwards. This offers fine views westwards, becoming obscured by bushes further downhill. The path runs beside the Hotel Rural El Refugio to reach **Cruz de Tejeda**, around 1510m (4955ft). Across the road is a larger hotel, the Parador. Walks 7, 8, 25, 42 and 43 start or finish here.

A stone cross in front of the Parador hotel at Cruz de Tejeda

Also present near the hotels is a row of covered souvenir stalls. Face these and go down stone steps just to the right, among pines and chestnuts. The old path is rather rugged, but an easier path has been trodden parallel downhill. Cross a road and continue down a pleasant and direct grassy path, past broom and tagasaste. Further down, the path is quite convoluted across rocky slopes.

Land on the road and turn right to the Km22 marker. Turn left down past houses at **Hoya de la Montaña**, on a concrete path with steps, then a stone-paved path, then a steep concrete track. Another path leads down to a road bend, where a shop and the Bar

47

Looking down on the scattered settlement of Las Lagunetas from an old path

Restaurante Perera lie to the left. Turn right, however, to walk up the road to the Km21 marker.

Look for a narrow, grassy path between houses, crossing a slope, giving way to a concrete path past more houses. Steps lead down to the road beside a house called **La Estanco**. Go through a gap in a roadside barrier, down a short path and down a steep concrete track. A winding path continues down to a road. Turn left down the road and left down a grassy track to a lower road in **Las Lagunetas**, just over 1100m (3610ft).

Turn right up the road, which steepens and often has a view of a church ahead. When a T junction is reached at a wayside shrine, either turn right to walk to a roundabout on the main road, or turn left, then right up steps to reach the church. If going to the church, turn right to follow a road away from it to the roundabout. Buses stop at the roundabout, otherwise follow the road gently downhill to return to the bus shelter tucked into the Barranco de la Mina.

WALK 4
Santa Brígida to Teror

Start	Santa Brígida
Finish	Teror
Distance	12km (7½ miles)
Total Ascent	550m (1805ft)
Total Descent	450m (1475ft)
Time	4hrs
Terrain	Mostly tarmac and concrete roads, steep at times, with linking stretches along farm tracks and old paths.
Refreshments	Bars at Santa Brígida, El Barranquillo and Teror.
Transport	Regular daily buses serve Santa Brígida and Teror from Las Palmas. Occasional buses link Santa Brígida and Pino Santo.

On 8 September every year, pilgrims walk from Santa Brígida to Teror, to reach the basilica of Nuestra Señora del Pino. The route they follow is partly signposted as the 'Pa'l Pino'. The final stage, from Caldera de Pino Santo, is shared with Walk 5 from San Mateo to Teror.

Start at a busy central road junction in **Santa Brígida** (shops, bars, post office, banks with ATMs, buses and taxis). Follow the Calle Real, a quiet and quaint street lined with bushes in pots. Notice the first 'Pa'l Pino' ceramic plaque mounted on a wall. The route turns left down Calle Muro, but first it is worth exploring around the church. ▶

Walk down the brick-paved Calle Muro and admire cacti planted below the balcony. Turn left as marked 'Pa'l Pino' down a steep, winding concrete track, continuing down a cobbly path. Cross the Barranco de Santa Brígida and turn left as signposted up a short, steep track. ▶ Reach a road at a house called Villa El Drago, although its dragon tree is dead.

Route uses SL 12 – 'Pa'l Pino'.

A balcony overlooks the route and three church bells – La Grande, La Ronca and La Chica – can be studied closely.

Walk 1 goes down the barranco.

49

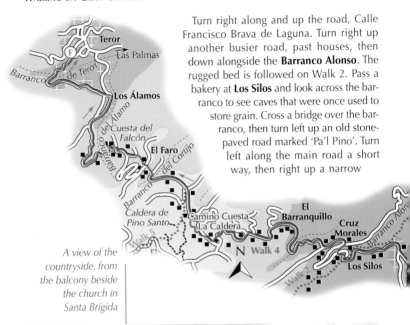

Turn right along and up the road, Calle Francisco Brava de Laguna. Turn right up another busier road, past houses, then down alongside the **Barranco Alonso**. The rugged bed is followed on Walk 2. Pass a bakery at **Los Silos** and look across the barranco to see caves that were once used to store grain. Cross a bridge over the barranco, then turn left up an old stone-paved road marked 'Pa'l Pino'. Turn left along the main road a short way, then right up a narrow

A view of the countryside, from the balcony beside the church in Santa Brígida

50

path zigzagging up a steep and scrubby slope. Turn right along the road to reach a seating area and a cross at **Cruz Morales**. This is a good viewpoint as it straddles a crest.

Turn left up the road, as signposted for Pino Santo. Turn right at another junction, also signposted for Pino Santo. The road runs downhill and overlooks a green and fertile barranco. The road crosses it and climbs to **El Barranquillo**, where the Bar Santo Pino is located. Continue up the road, later turning left as signposted for Pino Santo Alto. This road climbs for some distance, but eventually drops to a dip where there is a bus shelter. Before reaching the shelter, turn right around the wall of a house, spotting a marker for the 'Pa'l Pino'. In quick succession come a concrete track, grassy path and stone-paved path, reaching a road.

The basilica in Teror is the end of the trail for pilgrims from Santa Brígida and San Mateo

Turn left and climb steeply up the road, **Camino Cuesta La Caldera**. Branch left as marked up a steep concrete track. Continue up a path that is often trodden to bare, lumpy bedrock. Turn right at a house at the top and follow a short track to another house beside a road. Turn left to see the last 'Pa'l Pino' ceramic plaque fixed to the wall. Follow the road gently down and uphill, reaching a signposted crossroads, where this route joins the pilgrim route from San Mateo. Walk straight ahead down the only road without a signpost, and refer to Walk 5 for the route to Teror.

WALK 5
San Mateo to Teror

Start	San Mateo
Finish	Teror
Distance	11km (7 miles)
Total Ascent	450m (1475ft)
Total Descent	675m (2215ft)
Time	4hrs
Terrain	Mostly tarmac and concrete roads, steep at times, with linking stretches along farm tracks and old paths.
Refreshments	Plenty of choice in San Mateo and Teror.
Transport	Regular daily buses serve San Mateo and Teror from Las Palmas. Daily buses also link San Mateo, Utiaca and Teror.

On 8 September every year, pilgrims walk northwards from San Mateo to Teror, to the basilica of Nuestra Señora del Pino. They celebrate the day an image of the Virgin appeared in a pine tree in 1465. Much of the old trail is now along roads, but some interesting old paths remain.

The old part of the village, whose full name is Vega de San Mateo, is well worth exploring and is centred on the Plaza de Nuestra Señora del Pino (shops, bar/restaurants, banks with ATMs, post office, bus station and taxis). A small tourist information office offers information about walking routes in the area, which are marked very sparsely with paint.

Head for the centre of **San Mateo**, the Plaza de Nuestra Señora del Pino, around 825m (2705ft). Go behind the church and walk down Calle Lourdes to reach the little chapel of the Inmaculada. Turn right to drop straight into a barranco and climb from it along a steep concrete road. This levels out then later climbs to a road at the Restaurante Alcorac.

Turn right to follow the bendy road downhill, avoiding turnings along lesser roads. Go through a sheer-sided rock cutting and enjoy fine views of the **Barranco de la Mina**. Watch for a gap in the roadside barrier on the right, where a grassy, old, stone-paved path slices across a concrete buttress supporting the road. The path reaches a bend on a track, and the track runs down to a farm. Watch carefully for a path dropping to the right, down from the farm, between cane thickets and almond trees, to reach a track around 725m (2380ft). ▶

This is part of the PR GC 02, used in Walk 2.

Turn left a short way up the track, then right to cross a streambed. Walk up a concrete track to some houses. Turn left up a path, right up another path, passing houses all the way and climbing to a road in the village of **Utiaca**. ▶ Turn right along the road, gently down and up, passing houses and overlooking terraces. Pass **El Lomito** and continue up to a well-signposted crossroads on a crest in the village of **La Solana**. ▶

Turn left if a bar is required.

Turn right if a shop or bar is required.

Keep straight ahead up a short concrete road, then turn left down a broad, vegetated path to a road. Turn left again, turning right across a valley and up the other side. Go straight past houses on Lomo de los Corraletes and down a road. A tree stands in the middle of a triangular road junction on the left, and a concrete road winds steeply uphill. This is the **Cuesta del Piquillo**, punishingly steep, mostly flanked by prickly pears, aloes and incienso. Take a break at a complex, signposted road junction at the top, at almost 900m (2950ft). Views from both sides of a gap are good, revealing a well-populated countryside stretching from the coast to the mountains.

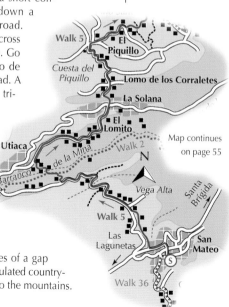

Map continues on page 55

53

The view of the Barranco de la Mina and Utiaca from the road through El Lomito

Take the road signposted for **El Piquillo**. Walk along and down the road, then down a concrete road and concrete path to a huddle of houses. Watch for a terrace path on the left, narrow and gravelly, with street lights alongside, as well as a narrow water channel. Cross a concrete road and walk down past one building, then turn left along another path. This runs down between terraces and occasional buildings, then once it rises, turn left to climb a concrete path. This becomes a track passing a few houses.

Before the track descends steeply, watch carefully to spot a path climbing to the left, between prickly pears. This is steep and rocky for a short way, then much easier, apparently approaching a splendid ruin. In fact, only half the building is ruined, and the other half is the Casa Rural La Caldera. Follow its access track to a road, noting the **Caldera de Pino Santo** to the left. This volcanic crater is fertile, supporting a citrus grove and fields. ▸

Turn right down the road to reach a crossroads. Turn left down the only road without a signpost. ▸ This becomes a concrete road down into the **Barranco del Cortijo**. Next, follow the road uphill, but turn left up a cobbled path, and link with a steep, winding concrete road up to a hamlet on a ridge at **El Faro**. Go straight across a road and down a concrete path, a zigzag with a few steps, reaching a road bend. Another stretch of concrete path continues on the right, giving way to a cobbled path down to a concrete road. The road, **Cuesta del Falcón**, drops very steeply, broadening and switching to tarmac.

Some maps wrongly show it as a lake.

Walk 4 joins here.

55

A half-ruined building of some character near the Caldera de Pino Santo

Follow the road down across the **Barranco del Álamo** and continue down to the village of **Los Álamos**, passing the Plaza de Igualdad. Walk straight down the Camino Real del Álamo. Turn left along Paseo La Ligüeña, which continues as Paseo de Florian, crossing the cane-choked Barranco de Teror. Walk up Calle El Chorrito and cross a busy road, heading straight for the basilica in the middle of **Teror**.

Pilgrims head for Nuestra Señora del Pino (bars, restaurants, banks with ATMs, post office and plenty of shops), where the domed basilica is surrounded by fine streets and plazas, and there are several tall trees nearby. To catch a bus, walk straight away from the door of the basilica, along Calle Real de la Plaza, which is flanked by houses with balconies. Turn left at the end, then right to find the little bus station. There are also taxis.

WALK 6

Pico de Bandama and Caldera de Bandama

Start/Finish	Casas de la Caldera, Bandama
Distance	8km (5 miles)
Total Ascent/Descent	275m (900ft)
Time	3hrs
Terrain	One short road walk, but mostly steep ash paths, on slopes of dense scrub.
Refreshments	Bar at Casas de la Caldera and on Pico de Bandama.
Transport	Regular daily buses serve Bandama from Las Palmas and Santa Brígida.

This is a highly convoluted, popular short walk that basically climbs to a mountain viewpoint and descends into a volcanic crater (caldera). Most of the steep slopes are eased by following a spiral road and zigzag paths. The name 'Bandama' derives from a 16th-century Flemish settler called 'Van Damme'.

Start at **Bandama**, where the bus reaches a gap between Pico de Bandama and the Caldera de Bandama, at a huddle of houses called **Casas de la Caldera**. There is a road junction on the gap, and a road signposted for 'Pico Bandama', with a 0km marker alongside. An ash path rises from the marker, but quickly turns left. Take care as the path is narrow and squeezes past dense scrub. Beware of aloes and prickly pears, and the latex sap from broken tabaibal. Later, keep right and climb more steeply, reaching a road at some chevron markers and a pine.

Turn right up the road, with a view into the crater, and keep spiralling up to a roundabout and a final peak of ash on Pico de Bandama. There is a viewing platform and a white building on the 574m (1883ft) summit. Views stretch from Las Palmas and the coast to the high mountains. Walk back down the spiral road and pass La Caldera restaurant and the Mirador del Vino.

When houses come into view ahead, turn sharp left through a gap in the roadside barrier, where there is volcanic ash and concrete blocks. Go down an ash path on a steep and scrubby slope, bending right to reach a gap. Follow a path up and down, over and over again, like a roller-coaster, ending with a more pronounced gap. Climb steeply to some dragon trees beside a golf course. Walk past the Vik Hotel Bandama Golf, turning right to follow its access road back to Casas de la Caldera and its bar.

A signpost for Caldera de Bandama points down through a gateway, open 0800 to 1700, with a viewpoint off to the right. Go down an attractively cobbled path flanked by walls, then crunch down an ash path to a small viewpoint. Keep heading downhill, sometimes with stone paving, reaching an *era* (circular threshing floor), ruins and a couple of tall eucalyptus. ◀

A water tap might be in working order.

Looking down on the Casas de la Caldera and golf course from Pico de Bandama

Aim to complete a circular walk around the base of the crater, or Caldera de Bandama, whose lowest point is 216m (709ft). Turn left to do this in a clockwise direction, passing a building and vegetable plots, passing another ruin and era, located among more eucalyptus. When the circuit is complete, retrace steps back uphill to Casas de la Caldera. If it is hot and frequent breaks are taken, admire the trees, bushy broom, aloes, prickly pears and tabaibal, while the lower scrub is scented with lavender and incienso.

Rugged lumps of rock are passed while walking round the rim of the Caldera de Bandama

59

VALLESECO AND TEROR

Yellow flowers of clover on a gentle slope, with Pico de Osorio rising as a dark hump beyond (Walk 10)

An interesting network of signposted and waymarked PR (pequeño recorrido) routes stretch all the way from the high mountains around Cruz de Tejeda, down into the deep, green and lush Barranco de la Virgen. Most walkers would prefer to follow routes downhill, one-way from Cruz de Tejeda to the villages of Teror and Valleseco. Climbing uphill would involve ascents exceeding 1000m (3280ft), on paths that are steep in places, which would prove difficult on hot and humid days.

On the lower slopes, a series of inter-linked, signposted and waymarked trails allow a couple of interesting circular walks between small villages, hamlets and farms, as well as the option to climb Pico de Osorio. Splendid bus services, running early until late, allow these walks to be started from the recreational area of La Laguna, although there is also the option to link these walks with the little town of Teror, using an old mule path that has survived being cut several times by a modern, zigzag main road.

Walks in this section can be linked with other routes in the high mountains, from Cruz de Tejeda, as well as with pilgrim trails serving Teror on the lower slopes, from the villages of Santa Brígida and San Mateo.

WALK 7
Cruz de Tejeda to Teror

Start	Cruz de Tejeda
Finish	Teror
Distance	12km (7½ miles)
Total Ascent	200m (655ft)
Total Descent	1120m (3675ft)
Time	3hrs 30mins
Terrain	Mostly downhill on forest paths and farm tracks, with some road-walking.
Refreshments	Bars at Cruz de Tejeda, El Lomo and Teror.
Transport	Occasional daily buses serve Cruz de Tejeda from Maspalomas and San Mateo. Regular daily buses from Teror to San Mateo and Las Palmas.

Apart from an initial climb from Cruz de Tejeda, over the shoulder of a mountain, this old route runs mostly downhill, through dense forest and mixed farmland. A walk through the deep-cut Barranco del Charquillo Madrelagua is followed by a short-cut through a bendy main road to reach Teror.

Start at the hotels at **Cruz de Tejeda**, around 1510m (4955ft), following the 'parking' sign. There are two mapboards beside the car park: one for the PR GC 01, the other for PR GC 04 (Walk 8). The path is stone-paved at first, and well trodden throughout as it climbs a slope of broom grazed by sheep and goats. There are views of Pico de las Nieves and Roque Nublo. The path undulates across the slope and reaches a road beside a pylon at **Cruz de Constantino**, over 1610m (5280ft).

Cross the road and drop into pine forest. Some parts of the path feature old boulder paving and the bedrock is a coarse conglomerate. There are a few large boulders near the path, as well as

Route uses PR GC 01.

Map continues on page 63

A rugged path descends through pine forest on the way towards Cuevas del Corcho

gnarled buttresses in the **Barranco de los Peñones**. Here there is a view of distant Las Palmas. The path surface becomes gentler further down, passing between a small field and a lumpy outcrop to reach a road at **Cuevas del Corcho**, around 1320m (4330ft). ◄ Turn right, noticing an aqueduct arch spanning an adjoining road.

There is a bus service here for Las Palmas, Teror and Artenara.

Go up a stone-paved ramp and continue a short way up into pine forest to cross a gap. The path is often worn into a groove or cut into the bedrock, and it later steps across the forested crest. When it emerges from the forest, an old farmhouse is seen in a fertile hollow at **Las**

Map continues
on page 65

Calderetas, where there are small ash cones. Pass a lava-dero, with water gushing through it, and follow a track to a concrete road, which descends towards the village of **Lanzarote**. When the road bends sharply left, keep straight ahead along an ash track, which later drops to a road, signpost and map-board.

The village of Lanzarote stands at an altitude of around 1100m (3610ft)

63

Continue straight along the road, passing the communal wash-place of Lavaderos de Tierras Blancas. Go gently down the road to a junction, where there is a fine stone-built **mirador**. Go up and down the Madrelagua road, and later straight ahead as signposted 'centro urbano'. Pass a couple of small lavaderos and the Bar Restaurante El Lomo to reach a three-way signpost, around 1050m (3445ft). ◄

There is a glimpse of Las Palmas here.

Turn right for Teror, not along a concrete path, but down an earth path. This takes a remarkable course downhill, bending several times to reveal ever-changing views into the steep-sided **Barranco del Charquillo Madrelagua**. Steep slopes of rampant scrub bear tagasaste trees before a road is reached. Turn left down the road, and tarmac gives way to concrete. A path crosses a footbridge then

A stone-paved path deep in the Barranco del Charquillo Madrelagua

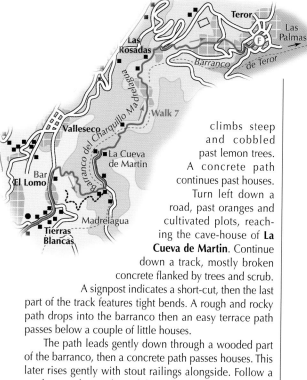

climbs steep and cobbled past lemon trees. A concrete path continues past houses. Turn left down a road, past oranges and cultivated plots, reaching the cave-house of **La Cueva de Martin**. Continue down a track, mostly broken concrete flanked by trees and scrub. A signpost indicates a short-cut, then the last part of the track features tight bends. A rough and rocky path drops into the barranco then an easy terrace path passes below a couple of little houses.

The path leads gently down through a wooded part of the barranco, then a concrete path passes houses. This later rises gently with stout railings alongside. Follow a road onwards, gently undulating across the valley side, passing houses at **Las Rosadas**. A signpost and map-board are reached on a busy main road bend.

Turn right down the road, watching for a signpost on the right, revealing a concrete road running downhill. This is the Camino Lugar Cuesta Los Estanques. It reaches houses, and a right turn further downhill is followed by a left turn along a level road. Go straight down Calle Isla de Gran Canaria until a busy road is reached. Turn right down this, and later left, into **Teror**. Head for the domed basilica of Nuestra Señora del Pino in the centre. ▶

See the end of Walk 5 for information about Teror.

WALK 8

Cruz de Tejeda to Valleseco

Start	Cruz de Tejeda
Finish	Valleseco
Distance	12km (7½ miles)
Total Ascent	510m (1675ft)
Total Descent	1070m (3510ft)
Time	4hrs
Terrain	Mostly downhill, but some steep climbs too, on forest paths and farm tracks, with some road-walking.
Refreshments	Bars at Cruz de Tejeda, Valsendero and Valleseco.
Transport	Occasional daily buses serve Cruz de Tejeda from Maspalomas and San Mateo. Regular daily buses from Valleseco to Teror, for Las Palmas.

This route runs very roughly parallel to Walk 7, crossing a mountain shoulder and descending through forest to the village of Valsendero. Winding tracks and roads cross over to Valleseco, overlooking cultivated countryside. Short road walks from Valleseco would easily link with Walks 7, 9 and 10.

Route includes PR GC 04 and PR GC 05.

Start at the hotels at **Cruz de Tejeda**, around 1510m (4955ft), following the 'parking' sign. There are two map-boards beside the car park: one for the PR GC 04, the other for PR GC 01 (Walk 7). The path climbs steeply beside pines and is worn to bedrock. Keep left of a small stone-built reservoir, climb past more pines, then make a fine traverse across a steep slope. There are rugged pinnacles of rock nearby, with Tejeda and Roque Nublo further away. The slope is grazed by sheep and goats, while the path exploits a soft red layer. A short descent leads to a road and signposts, where a left turn leads quickly to a viewpoint shelter at 1660m (5446ft) on **Degollada de las Palomas**.

The PR GC 04 is signposted up stone steps and a well-worn path, heading into pines and over a rise before

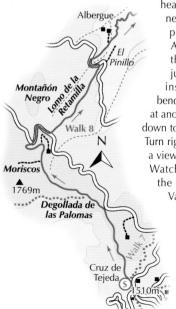

heading down to a track near **Moriscos**. A signpost points left for Artenara, but follow the track down to a junction and turn right instead. The track is bendy, and by keeping left at another junction it winds down to a road and signpost. Turn right, round a bend, for a view of **Montañón Negro**. Watch for a signpost on the left of the road for Valsendero.

The path is level and indistinct at first, passing burnt pines, but becomes clearer. Follow it down from

Cloud drifts across the high mountain crest on the way to Degollada de las Palomas

Map continues on page 68

67

the forest and along the grassy, broomy crest of **Lomo de la Retamilla**, passing a roofless ruin. Level out among tall eucalyptus and go down past pines and chestnuts hung with straggly lichen, reaching a road bend near a gateway to **El Pinillo**. Turn left up the road and cross a small bridge, then turn right as signposted down a track into a valley. Pass more chestnuts hung with straggly lichen, then pass a grassy space and a couple of gateways – the latter marked '**Albergue y Comedor**'.

The compact little village of Valsendero, seen while climbing towards Tres Piedras

Turn right at a track junction, signposted as the PR GC 04 down to Valsendero. This is rough and stony, broad and winding, dropping past rampant, bramble-tangled scrub, patches of woodland, occasional buildings and cultivated plots. Turn left downhill twice at junctions, then there is an uphill stretch, flashed yellow/white. Turn right downhill as signposted on a steep and winding concrete track. This becomes a tarmac road down past houses to a map-board and signpost above the village of **Valsendero**. ▶

Walk down the road to reach a bar and link with Walk 9.

Turn right as signposted for the PR GC 05 to Valleseco, down and up a track, passing a notice about an old mill. Climb the steep and winding concrete Camino La Cuesta, overlooking Valsendero and the Barranco de La Virgen. Keep left twice, climbing all the time round sweeping bends, reaching the top at **Mirador de las Tres Piedras**. ▶ Turn right up the track to a road and signpost, then turn left down the road to a farm. Turn right as signposted at the last building, up a narrow path. Watch for a right turn up another narrow path, through tagasaste bushes, to a hilltop **cross** at 1100m (3610ft), overlooking the valley and distant Las Palmas.

Las Palmas can be seen in the distance.

Walk back down the path and turn right along a track a short way, then right again down a winding, stone-paved path flanked by prickly pears. The last bit is a steep and curved concrete track down to a road, map-board and signposts. Cross the road and walk down a sunken, walled path, then follow a track to a road and signpost. Turn left down the road, Calle Parroco Marrero Díaz, and turn right at the bottom along Calle Perojo. Turn left down Calle Leon y Castillo, signposted 'centro urbano', for the centre of **Valleseco**, around 950m (3115ft) (shops, bars, banks with ATMs, post office, buses, taxis and tourist information office).

WALK 9
Cruz de La Laguna and Valsendero

Start/Finish	Cruz de La Laguna
Alternative Finish	Teror
Distance	12km (7½ miles); to Teror: 14km (8¾ miles)
Total Ascent/Descent	600m (1970ft); extra descent to Teror: 275m (900ft)
Time	4hrs; to Teror: 5hrs
Terrain	Roads, farm tracks and old paths, sometimes level and sometimes very steep, in and out of barrancos in a well-settled area.
Refreshments	Restaurant at Cruz de La Laguna. Bar off-route at Valsendero.
Transport	Daily buses serve Cruz de La Laguna from Teror and Valleseco. Regular daily buses link Teror and Las Palmas.

This circuit follows three waymarked trails, each made up of roads, farm tracks and old mule paths. Overall, the route descends from the recreational area of La Laguna, deep into the Barranco de La Virgen, then climbs back. It is possible to extend the walk and finish down in Teror.

Route uses SL 02, SL 03 and PR GC 06.

Start at **Cruz de La Laguna**, at almost 900m (2950ft), and the only place on the walk with buses. Follow the Valleseco road from the Restaurante Los Arcos. A signpost on the right indicates the SL 02 for the Barranco de La Virgen. Go down a narrow road and up through a valley planted with lemons. Walk straight ahead at a junction, down another road. Climb steeply from a junction, as signposted for **Zamora**. Turn right at the top of the road, then left down a concrete track, following SL 02 signposts.

A concrete path flanked by lamp-posts leads gently down into a fertile valley. Turn right at the bottom along an earth path beside a streambed. Cross over it and climb another concrete path, keeping left of two houses while bending left and right up to a junction with a concrete track. Turn left and climb steeply, levelling out to meet a tarmac road.

Turn right as signposted, gently down and up the bendy road. Pass the neighbourhoods of Troyanas and **Carpinteras**, almost touching 1000m (3280ft) while overlooking barrancos with wooded areas, mixed scrub and cultivated plots. As the road runs gently downhill, watch carefully for the SL 02 signposted up to the left. A narrow terrace path leads to a junction. Turning right leads back to the road, so turn left down the other path, winding easily down steep and rugged slopes, overlooking the Barranco de La Virgen. Pass a little house and go down steps to a road.

Turn left through a cutting, then right as signposted down steps to another little house. The path wriggles beneath an aqueduct pipeline four times then follows a water channel a short way. Continue on a downward traverse across the valley side, into chestnut woods, then down to a road, where there is a map-board and signpost near **El Cercado**, around 800m (2625ft). Turning left up the road leads quickly to the village of **Valsendero**. ▶ However, turn right to continue the walk.

Out of sight, but offers a bar.

The road runs down through the **Barranco de La Virgen** as the SL 03. Notices to right and left point out where remnants of laurisilva forest are located, otherwise the most notable features are groves of oranges and lemons, rampant scrub, the steep flanks of the barranco and fine houses along the way. The tarmac runs out and a broad dirt road

map continues on page 74

71

continues through the barranco, reaching another map-board and signpost on the right, around 600m (1970ft). At this point, the PR GC 06 leads back to La Laguna.

A narrow, cobbled path descends from the road, then climbs past a tall pine near a couple of houses. There is another trail-side notice about laurisilva, then climb to a house and turn left up its access track. This winds as it climbs, offering views further down the barranco. ◄ A road-end is reached at **Puerta de la Montaña**, where people once paid a tax to enter and exploit the forest of Doramas, now barely a shadow of its former self.

Climb the steep road, which is flanked by heather trees, while a notice on the right explains about two mills that once operated here – El Molinete and El Molino de Abajo. ◄ Follow the road uphill, then down to cross a streambed, and keep left to climb a steep road past the little chapel of La Virgen de la Silla. Note the huddle of typical Canarian tiled roofs while passing.

Climb to a crossroads and keep straight ahead up a very steep road on **Lomo de los Pinos**, where most of the trees are eucalyptus. The gradient eases, while a roadside notice explains about the neighbourhoods of Caserón,

Explored on Walk 10.

The mill race is the water channel with steps alongside.

A notice-board deep in the Barranco de la Virgen, before the climb to Puerta de la Montaña

Carpinteras and Troyanas, which were formerly estates. Views reveal the barranco to be both well-wooded and well-settled.

Follow the road across a dip, then turn left twice in quick succession at a wayside cross. Go down a bendy road past houses, and turn right at a junction along another road. However, quickly turn left up a concrete track. A broad grassy path continues straight ahead, zig-zagging up to a slope of chestnut trees. There is a notice about the Zamora and Sobradilla neighbourhoods, as well as views towards the high mountains.

Cross a road as signposted and follow another broad path up to a track junction. Keep straight ahead, following a track flanked by tall fences. The recreational area of **La Laguna** lies to the left, around 875m (2870ft). This shallow crater is surrounded by a fence that has a couple of gateways allowing access. An easy, level, circular walk is available between an outer circle of pines and an inner circle of heather trees. The central area is largely replanted laurisilva, where a shallow pond attracts a

Looking across typical Canarian tiled roof-tops from the little chapel of La Virgen de la Silla

73

variety of birds. Either turn left along a road to enter the site, or turn right to return to the road junction at **Cruz de La Laguna** to finish.

Alternative finish at Teror

A signpost for Teror points down a road near one of the access gates for La Laguna. It drops quickly to the exceptionally bendy main road. Cross the road directly four times, passing eucalyptus, pines and vegetable plots. Next time, head left along the road to find a short path clipping a road bend. The next path is long and cobbled, flanked by brambles, then a concrete track leads down to the road. Cross again and pass a sports stadium. Turn right down the main road, then keep straight ahead down the quiet Camino de Castaño. This drops more and more steeply, then turn right down Calle de la Herreria, concrete and brick-paved, into **Teror**. ◄

For services here, see the end of Walk 5.

An old path, predating the winding main road, offers an alternative finish down to Teror

WALK 10
Cruz de La Laguna and Las Madres

Start/Finish	Cruz de La Laguna
Alternative Finish	Teror
Distance	13km (8 miles); to Teror: 15km (9½ miles)
Total Ascent/Descent	500m (1640ft); extra descent to Teror: 275m (900ft)
Time	4hrs 30mins; to Teror: 5hrs 15mins
Terrain	Roads, farm tracks and old paths, sometimes level and sometimes steep, in and out of barrancos in a well-settled area.
Refreshments	Restaurants at Cruz de La Laguna and Los Chorros.
Transport	Daily buses serve Cruz de La Laguna from Teror and Valleseco. Occasional buses serve Los Chorros. Regular daily buses link Teror and Las Palmas.

This route shares its first stage, a descent into the Barranco de La Virgen, in common with Walk 9. Another path, the Vueltos del Camello, is used to climb out of the barranco from Las Madres. On the return to La Laguna, Pico de Osorio can be climbed, and the route can also be extended down to Teror.

Start at **Cruz de La Laguna**, at almost 900m (2950ft), and follow a road towards **La Laguna**, over a rise beside a football ground. A house is reached at a road junction, where a map-board and signposts indicate the PR GC 06, to the left, and PR GC 07, to the right. The former is used on the outward journey and the latter on the return. Turn left and follow the road, then turn left down a broad path and cross a road. Zigzag down a slope of chestnuts, look at a notice about the Zamora and Sobradilla neighbourhoods, and take in views to the high mountains.

Go straight down a grassy path and concrete track. Turn quickly right and left by road, as signposted and marked. Go along and up the road to a wayside cross, then turn right twice in quick succession to follow a road

Route uses PR GC 06, SL 03 and PR GC 07.

across a dip. Walk over a rise, passing a notice explaining about the neighbourhoods of Caserón, Carpinteras and Troyanas, which were formerly estates. Views reveal the barranco to be both well-wooded and well-settled. Go down an increasingly steep road on **Lomo de los Pinos**, where most of the trees are eucalyptus, and continue straight down through a crossroads.

The road drops steeply past the little chapel of La Virgen de la Silla. Note the huddle of typical Canarian tiled roofs while passing. Keep right as signposted at a road junction, across a couple of streambeds, up and down Calle El Molinete. A notice on the left explains about two mills which once operated here – El Molinete and El Molino de Abajo. ◄ A road-end is reached at **Puerta de la Montaña**, where people once paid a tax to enter and exploit the forest of Doramas, now barely a shadow of its former self.

Wind steeply down a track, passing a house and looking down into the barranco. The path downhill passes a notice about laurisilva and is cobbled. It later passes a tall pine near a couple of houses, then climbs

The mill race is the water channel with steps alongside.

The view of the Barranco de La Virgen on the descent from Puerta de la Montaña

to a dirt road, map-board and signposts in the **Barranco de La Virgen**, around 600m (1970ft). ▶ Turn sharp right down the road, via the SL 03, passing oranges and lemons before winding down through pine forest to a concrete turning space and the start of a tarmac road at **Las Madres**. There is a map-board and signpost.

Turn right for the PR GC 07, up a steep concrete road and gentler tarmac road, until barred by a green gate. Turn left along a short concrete track to a house, and continue up a narrow, stone-paved path, meandering on a steep slope. Keep right at two junctions, always climbing the clearest path. Pass a mirador on **Vueltas del Camello**, beside a tall eucalyptus on a steep slope of tangled scrub. When a house is reached, follow its concrete access track up to a tarmac road and PR GC 07 signpost. Turn left up

Left up the road leads, via Walk 9, towards Valsendero and Walk 8.

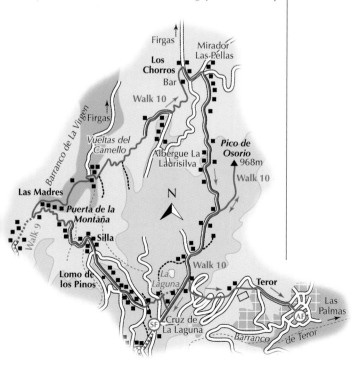

77

WALKING ON GRAN CANARIA

A path-side notice-board at the mirador on the Vueltas del Camello

the road, then right down a concrete track beside a stand of eucalyptus.

A winding earth track crosses a valley bottom and continues among pines, generally climbing to a stout gateway where a tarmac access road continues uphill past eucalyptus. The road later drops and bends right, so keep straight ahead down a clear path as signposted. A worn groove bends and becomes a fine stone-paved path beside chestnuts. Climb beside a few tall oaks and pass a notice about a spring at **Los Chorros**. Follow a track past bramble-tangled tagasaste, broom and calcosas, fragrant with incienso. Head gently downhill beside eucalyptus, to a road and signpost.

Turn sharp right up the road, which can be busy, but only follow it to a junction at Meson Los Chorros, and turn left as signposted for Teror and La Laguna. Go down the road, turning right and quickly right again at the **Mirador Las Pellas** and El Marchante restaurant. ◀ Climb

There is a view of Las Palmas and La Isleta.

steeply up a quiet road, cross a dip and pass a signpost. Slopes have been planted to regenerate laurisilva forest, and the **Albergue La Laurisilva** is passed.

Further up the road, on a slight gap near a white house, is a three-way signpost. Turn sharp left to follow a trodden earth path up through the laurisilva, on a few log steps. Cross a false summit and keep left, down along a crest, then keep straight ahead as signposted 'Camino al Pico', flanked by heather trees and incienso. Reach a trig point and small cross on **Pico de Osorio**, at 968m (3176ft). Enjoy the views then retrace steps to the road.

Follow the road onwards, up past Casa Pico de Osorio, then gently downhill and left at a junction. Reach a stout wall and fence surrounding the crater and recreational area at **La Laguna**, around 875m (2870ft). Follow the road straight back to **Cruz de La Laguna** to finish.

Alternative finish at Teror

If you wish to lengthen the walk, turn left as signposted for Teror and see the end of Walk 9 for the 2km (1¼ mile) descent to **Teror**.

A three-way signpost where a path can be followed along a forested crest onto Pico de Osorio

ARTENARA AND TAMADABA

The moist, forested uplands of Tamadaba supply small reservoirs, such as Presa de los Pérez (Walk 13)

Artenara is a splendid little village straddling a gap in mountains. It is served by only a few buses, and has limited lodgings, but its surroundings are well worth exploring. There is immediate access to a high, forested mountain called Moriscos, which can be climbed relatively easily for its own sake. However, there is also a long, interesting walk heading down through varied countryside to the low-lying town of Santa María de Guía. There are plenty of buses allowing a quick exit at the finish.

Artenara is very handy for walks around the remote forested uplands of Tamadaba, and there are plenty of signposts and waymarks. In this section, Walk 12 makes its way from Artenara to Tamadaba, where there is a basic campsite. By referring to Walk 42 later in the book, another route allows a return to the village. It is also possible to enjoy a splendid circular walk around Tamadaba from the low-lying village of San Pedro, linking old mule paths.

The fertile plateau of Vega de Acusa also lies in this area. It has no bus service, but can be approached from Artenara by walkers without cars. A short circular walk around the cliffs bounding the plateau reveal a series of interesting little cave houses. Walkers with cars can approach Acusa by following an exceptionally scenic and convoluted road from La Aldea.

WALK 11
Moriscos to Santa María de Guía

Start	Between Montañón Negro and Moriscos
Alternative Start	Pinos de Gáldar
Finish	Santa María de Guía
Distance	22km (13¾ miles); from Pinos de Gáldar: 17km (10½ miles)
Total Ascent	250m (820ft); from Pinos de Gáldar: 70m (230ft)
Total Descent	1830m (6005ft); from Pinos de Gáldar: 1650m (5415ft)
Time	7hrs; from Pinos de Gáldar: 5hrs
Terrain	An initial climb on forest tracks, followed by a long descent, steep at times, on roads, tracks and paths, through forest and farmland.
Refreshments	Bars at Lomo El Palo, Saucillo and Santa María de Guía.
Transport	Occasional daily buses pass Moriscos and Pinos de Gáldar from Las Palmas, Teror and Artenara. Occasional daily buses link Saucillo, Tegueste and Pineda with Gáldar.

Although this looks like a long walk, it is mostly downhill and mostly along easy roads, paths and tracks. The ascent of Moriscos can be omitted and the walk could be started later at Pinos de Gáldar. There are few buses to the start, so start as early as possible. However, there are plenty of buses at the end.

Start on a road bend between Montañón Negro and Moriscos, where a dirt road is signposted PR GC 04 to Cruz de Tejeda (Walk 8). Follow the bendy track up to a signposted junction and turn right as indicated for Artenara. Rise past another signposted junction, again ahead as if for Artenara. When yet another junction is reached, turn left past a chain barrier. Climb, bending right and left, passing a radome to reach a mast, trig point and fire tower at 1769m (5804ft) on **Moriscos**. Views are limited because of tall pines.

Walk back down the track, past the chain barrier, turning right to reach a signpost. Turn left, gently down

Route uses short stretches of PR GC 04 and SL 1.

an un-signposted track through pine forest. This steepens and ends suddenly, so go down a winding ash path on slope of broom at **Charco de la Arena**. Join a road around 1600m (5250ft) and turn left to follow it. The road is flanked by pines, then an ash path rises parallel on the right, with a view of Altavista. Cross a forested crest and bare ash, heading down to a road junction. Go down a narrow road to another road junction and mirador at **Pinos de Gáldar**. There is a view of a volcanic crater dotted with a few pines. ◄

A short-cut on the map omits the viewpoint.

Alternative start at Pinos de Gáldar

The mirador offers an alternative starting point, with a very steep descent signposted as the SL 1.

The SL 1 from Pinos de Gáldar drops down a slope of soft ash covered in pine needles, flanked by drystone walls. The walls move closer together, then paths head left and right. Turn left, then immediately right to follow a well-trodden earth path, staying high. This soon follows a wall along a crest, with pines to the right and views to the left. The route crosses rounded, steep-sided, grassy hills.

Looking into a steep-sided crater from a viewpoint at Pinos de Gáldar

There are many animal paths, but follow the walker's path to a road, over

Map continues on page 84

Caserío Saucillo

Montaña Acebuche

Las Rosas

Caideros

■ *Montaña Buenaventura*

1200m (3940ft) at **Majadales**, where there is a signpost for the SL 1.

Llano de las Mesas

Risco Blanca

Bar **Lomo El Palo**

Walk 11

Majadales

Walk up the road, rising gently past pens for sheep and goats, passing the Bar Lomo El Palo and a recreational area. Go down the road and it levels out, swinging right. Go straight ahead along a grassy track through a tagasaste plantation. The track becomes concrete, so turn right gently down another track, and continue down a path. Link with a concrete track straight ahead down to a road, and continue roughly along and down a crest, with well-grazed slopes all around. Follow the bendy road down to a main road near **Montaña Buenaventura**, and cross over to walk straight down another road.

Los Galeotes

Pinos de Gáldar

N

Montañón del Capitán

1662m ▲ **Montañón Negro**

Artenara

Walk 8

Charco de la Arena

S

▲**Moriscos** → Teror

1769m

Pass a few houses and level out near **Las Rosas**. Turn left as marked by a yellow arrow and go up a concrete track to a pylon. Walk

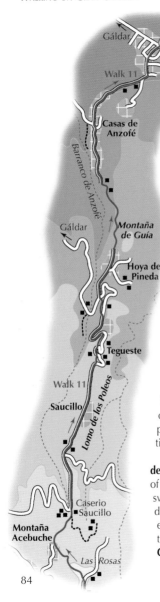

down across a slope covered in incienso, later looking down to the village of **Caideros**. Follow the track down through broom and tagasaste, to a gap where a few buildings and caves huddle together near **Montaña Acebuche**. Keep right, straight ahead, along a road. Keep right on a gap to follow a concrete path downhill. When the concrete climbs left, go down a stone-strewn path with masses of aloes and prickly pears above, keep right of a wall and fence, going down a narrow, stone-paved path. Go down a farm road and bend left to a road with a bus shelter beside it near **Caserio Saucillo**.

Turn right down the road, dropping below 800m (2625ft), through the village of **Saucillo**, passing the Bar Restaurante Pepe. The road runs gently along the **Lomo de los Poleos**, and, when it bends sharp right, go down a fenced path on the left to short-cut a bend. Further along the road, short-cut another bend at **Tegueste** by following a track and path past a house. Turn left down the road and turn a pronounced right-hand bend. When there is a deep gash in a cliff on the right, turn left through a gap in the roadside barrier, down a clear path. Quickly turn right and follow a narrow path down a scrubby slope, reaching a road junction and bus shelter.

Take the road signposted for the village of **Hoya de Pineda** and keep left, or straight ahead, to the end of the road. Continue down a short concrete path, switching to a narrow trodden path strewn with debris beneath an overhanging cliff. The path is easier along the stone-paved top of a pipeline. A track leads to houses and a road continues down to **Casas de Anzofé**. Keep right at the modern chapel

A path descends to a road, which is followed to a bar at Lomo El Palo

It is worth walking up cobbled streets to explore around the church.

of Santa Rita to walk further down the road, overlooking fertile land to the left, with El Teide and Tenerife far beyond, and Pico de Gáldar closer to hand. Turn left down past a severed mill race, cross a barranco and keep straight ahead to reach a road junction, over 100m (330ft) in the middle of **Santa María de Guía** (shops, bars, banks with ATMs, post office, buses and taxis). ◄

WALK 12
Artenara to Tamadaba

Start	Artenara
Finish	Campsite, Tamadaba
Distance	13km (8 miles); with extension: 17km (10½ miles)
Total Ascent	500m (1640ft); with extension: 800m (2625ft)
Total Descent	540m (1770ft); with extension: 840m (2755ft)
Time	4hrs; with extension: 5hrs 15mins
Terrain	Easy roads and tracks in cultivated valleys, with some steep paths through extensive pine forest.
Refreshments	Bars in Artenara.
Transport	Occasional daily buses serve Artenara from Las Palmas and Teror.

Tamadaba is a remote, but popular forested area with a campsite. Buses run to Artenara, leaving walkers with a number of options to reach the area. One route is described here, along with a spur route to the forested crest of Risco Faneque. Walk 42 can be used to return to Artenara immediately, or after camping overnight.

Route uses SL 10.

Start over 1200m (3940ft) in the centre of **Artenara** (pensión, bar/restaurants, bank, post office, buses and splendid viewpoints), where signposts indicate several destinations, including Tamadaba. Go down the main road to a roundabout on a gap and turn right as signposted for Las Cuevas and Agaete. Quickly turn left down a narrow road

Map continues
on page 89

signposted Chajunco, passing a map-board showing a route to San Pedro. Walk into a valley and up the other side, overlooking fertile terraces. Head round into another valley and walk up through **Las Cuevas**, admiring cave houses. Climb a steep concrete road, later gently rising and falling, then climb steeply to a junction.

Keep left, in effect straight ahead down the road for Lugarejos. A signpost down the road indicates an old 'camino' short-cutting a road bend. This stone-paved path later drops back to the road beside a small cross, **Cruz de Cazadores**, and another signpost. Continue straight ahead, along and down the road, reaching a three-way signpost at a concrete water store above **Coruña**. Head right, along a gentle terrace path (not the one with handrails). Join a concrete track at another three-way signpost, turning right for

Looking back along a narrow concrete track near Coruña, towards Moriscos

87

Lugarejos. Further down the track is another signpost, so head right along a rocky crest where boulders have been pushed aside. Wind down a stone-paved path into the **Barranco del Lugarejo**, to a three-way signpost.

Turning right leads to a bar, and by continuing through Lugarejos, Walk 13 can be joined at Presa de Lugarejos and followed to San Pedro.

Turn left, following a stone-paved path downstream, and cross a concrete slab bridge. Follow a concrete track to a junction and signpost, walking ahead. Go gently up and down to reach a junction with a concrete road. ◀ Turn left down the road, then left down a narrow path signposted as the SL 10. This runs beside a streambed, crosses a concrete slab bridge, then climbs on conglomerate bedrock. Turn left at the top and follow a concrete path below a cliff. Follow a road past caves and cave houses at **Las Hoyas**.

The Presa de Lugarejos is one of three little reservoirs in this area

Watch for a path down to the right, winding round a sunken house, down past terraces, reaching a concrete road that drops quickly to another road. Turn left then quickly head right, parallel to the road. A path leads to a concrete footbridge, below 900m (2950ft). Only cross half of this bridge, then climb straight up a crest between two barrancos. The slope is partly covered in pines, but mostly dense cistus with some tagasaste. There is bare rock part of the way, then a slight descent to cross a streambed. The

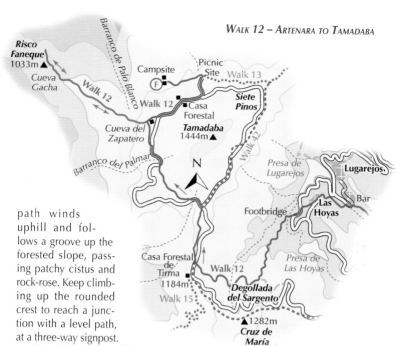

path winds
uphill and fol-
lows a groove up the
forested slope, pass-
ing patchy cistus and
rock-rose. Keep climb-
ing up the rounded
crest to reach a junc-
tion with a level path,
at a three-way signpost.

Turn right for Tamadaba,
and the path undulates among dense
pines crossing valleys and ridges before climbing
to a road just above a gap at Tirma, where there is another
three-way signpost. ▶ Cross the road and turn right for
Tamadaba, walking parallel to the road among pines,
rock-rose and asphodel, around 1200m (3940ft). Views
to the right include Moriscos and Roque Nublo, while
to the left, El Teide and Tenerife can be seen. The path
reaches another three-way signpost at a road junction.

Turn left to follow the road, watching on the right
for a signpost for Tamadaba. Follow a path, zigzagging at
first, then climbing among pines and rock-rose, traversing
high above the road. The slopes are quite rocky in places,
and the path comes down to the road at the head of the
Barranco del Palmar. Follow the road a short way, then
take a path to the left, traversing a slope below the road,
reaching a stone building at **Cueva del Zapatero**. Follow

Left quickly leads
to Casa Forestal
de Tirma, and the
start of Walk 15.

89

An extension is possible down a forested crest to Risco Faneque, returning the same way afterwards

a track up to a three-way signpost. If you wish to extend the walk down to Risco Faneque, turn left. Otherwise, keep right to climb on to the road.

Extension to Risco Faneque

From the three-way signpost, follow a path downhill and turn right. The path is broad and clear, descending through pine forest with heather trees in places, but mostly a ground cover of rock-rose. When the path forks, it quickly re-joins, becoming narrow and later dropping through a notch in a rock-step. Reach a gap and climb towards lumpy cliffs, keeping right to find a way up. There are slabby slopes, sparse pines, cistus and tabaibal. Enjoy views then retrace steps back to the three-way signpost. Keep left to rejoin the main route.

Turn left to follow the road past the **Casa Forestal** buildings, reaching a junction. Turn left down a patchy road, then right at a parking area in the forest, to follow a track past a picnic site, and so reach a **campsite** on a slope below 1200m (3940ft).

WALK 13
San Pedro and Tamadaba

Start/Finish	San Pedro
Distance	16km (10 miles)
Total Ascent/Descent	1200m (3940ft)
Time	5hrs 30mins
Terrain	Steep and rugged paths climb to gentler forest tracks and paths. Steep and stony descents, broken by easier roads and tracks.
Refreshments	Bars at San Pedro.
Transport	Regular daily buses from Las Palmas to Agaete. Taxi from Agaete to San Pedro.

A steep climb on a winding mountain path reaches an extensive pine forest. There are plenty of paths around Tamadaba, and the one chosen for the descent winds down to Presa de los Pérez. A series of steep and rugged paths lead down through a deep barranco to return to San Pedro.

Start in **San Pedro**, below 200m (655ft), at the Bar La Palma. Follow a road uphill signposted as the Camino Real Tamadaba. Pass the Bar Casa Tino and climb steeply to the road-end, then climb a stretch of concrete road. Pass a signpost and climb past the last couple of houses, up a winding path with street lights, past a big eucalyptus, onto a scrubby crest.

Climb into a steep-sided valley, with one slight downhill stretch, passing a few almond trees and a couple of palms. Cross a streambed and climb into a rocky gully, up bare-rock or a partly stone-paved path. There are amazing towers of rock above, and a cliff full of curious little caves. As the path climbs higher it is more likely to be stone-paved on crumbling ash beds, with feathery tussocks of grass and white tajinaste alongside. Reach a

Route uses SL 1.

A rugged, stone-paved path climbs high above San Pedro towards Roque Bermejo

Walk 41 joins from the right.

gap around 650m (2130ft), near **Roque Bermejo**, where there is an era and a signpost. ◄

Turn left as signposted for Tamadaba, climbing and catching a glimpse of the Anaga Peninsula of Tenerife. The path is narrow, but clear, passing tabaibal, cistus and bracken on slopes studded with big boulders. The cliffs above have no apparent breach, so the path is deflected to the right on a rising traverse until one appears. The path climbs through the breach and is stone-paved as it follows a rocky ridge, with cistus and rock-rose alongside. The final zigzags have stout buttresses, climbing to pine and eucalyptus as the path enters a forest, passing notices on **Montaña de las Presas**, over 1000m (3280ft).

Follow a gently undulating, but generally rising path through the forest, often cushioned with pine needles. Rise to a track and continue onwards and upwards. Always keep ahead and climb at junctions, no matter what other paths and tracks do. When the track does drop, at a number 7 marker, keep left to climb a clear, winding path. This becomes steep and stone-paved, with heather trees among pines, reaching a stony track. Turn right up the track, signposted for Artenara, and reach another signpost near a large **picnic site**, over 1200m (3940ft). ▶

The Tamadaba forest campsite lies off to the right.

93

A concrete channel is followed beside the Presa de los Pérez, then its dam is crossed

Straight ahead downhill leads to Lugarejos, but results in more road-walking later.

A path is signposted uphill for Artenara, rising and falling, but generally rising through dense pine forest hung with straggly skeins of lichen. Reach a three-way signpost below a road at **Siete Pinos**. Turn left downhill, signposted for El Hornillo, where laurisilva species have been planted among pines, and tall heather trees are present. Later, the path swings right and climbs gently across a crest. The way down the other side is more rugged, but broad and clear, often zigzagging. Reach another three-way signpost. ◄

Turn sharp left down a path that is narrow and stony, but abundantly clear as it zigzags down through the forest, often across boulder-strewn slopes. Walk beside a concrete channel next to **Presa de los Pérez**, around 850m (2790ft). Cross a dam to reach a road and another three-way signpost. Turn left to follow the road to a well-signposted crossroads, and keep left down a road leading to **El Hornillo**. There is a small paved plaza in front of an ermita, then a signpost for the SL 1, El Sao and Agaete.

Note cave houses on surrounding cliffs, while following a partly stone-paved path as it drops past little terraces. Climb a bit to cross a slight gap, then pass below overhanging cliffs with more caves. Aloes, almonds and tagasaste flank the path as it drops further, sometimes on bare rock. Climb from a barranco, past a three-way signpost, turning left down a stone-paved path past houses at **El Sao**, to a tarmac road and a signpost. Turn right down the road, then up to another signpost. A path heads left from the road, rugged underfoot, climbing as it passes three pylons. ▶ Zigzag down steep, rocky slope of pines, and note that the path doesn't hit the road at **Los Berrazales**, but is fenced between plots as it goes down steps, around 400m (1310ft).

There is a fine view down the barranco to Agaete.

Don't cross a concrete footbridge, but go down a stone-paved and trodden path, following a black plastic pipe along the barranco bed. Pass a signpost and go down and up a concrete road, to another signpost beside a tarmac road at **Casas del Camino**. Turn left and walk gently down the road to yet another signpost at a transformer tower. Go down a paved path with steps, past houses, then along a trodden path that is gritty and stony. Another paved path with steps leads from houses to a sports ground. Follow a track to the left, then continue to a road and turn right to cross a bridge to **San Pedro**, finishing at the Bar La Palma.

WALK 14

Artenara and Vega de Acusa

Start/Finish	Acusa Seca
Alternative Start/Finish	Artenara
Distance	7km (4½ miles); from Artenara: 15km (9½ miles)
Total Ascent/Descent	250m (820ft); from Artenara: 600m (1970ft)
Time	2hrs 30mins; from Artenara: 5hrs
Terrain	Mostly good tracks and roads, with a few rugged cliff paths. The descent from Artenara is mostly on forested slopes.
Refreshments	Bars at Artenara.
Transport	Occasional daily buses serve Artenara from Las Palmas and Teror.

Vega de Acusa is a cultivated plateau surrounded on most sides by sheer cliffs, with intriguing cave houses at Acusa Seca. A short circular walk is available to anyone arriving by car. Walkers using buses can start from Artenara and follow a route down to Vega de Acusa, returning afterwards.

Alternative start/finish at Artenara

If arriving by bus, start over 1200m (3940ft) in the centre of **Artenara** (pensión, bar/restaurants, bank, post office and splendid viewpoints), where signposts indicate several destinations. Go down the main road to a roundabout on a gap and walk straight up a road signposted cementerio. Turn left before the cemetery, as signposted along a track. Reach a junction of tracks beside a helipad. ◄

There are views of Pico de las Nieves, Roque Nublo and Roque Bentayga, as well as map-boards and signposts.

Turn left down a path signposted for Acusa, gently at first, across a steep slope of pines on **Brezos**, overlooking the deep Barranco de Tejeda. The path drops and winds more steeply, sometimes with stone paving, or worn into bedrock. There is a view of Vega de Acusa ahead – a fertile hump surrounded by mountains. The path runs in and out of

the forest, with tabaibal and tagasaste, as well as masses of lavender on sunny slopes.

Cross a track as signposted and cross a low, rugged hill, taking

a moment to spot the path down the other side. A bare rock groove, with bits of chunky old stone paving, winds down past sparse pines and lush scrub, again notable for the amount of lavender. Don't go down to a road and houses, but step up to the left as signposted for Acusa. The old path wanders through pines to reach another road and signpost. Turn left and follow the bendy road downhill with amazing views of the deep barranco, reaching a car park around 900m (2950ft), where the main circuit starts.

Looking down towards Vega de Acusa from Brezos, with Inagua rising beyond

Go down a stone-paved path and steps, winding past the entrances to several cave houses at **Acusa Seca**. Cliffs overhang and the path becomes more rugged, climbing crude stone steps to El Alamo. The path becomes gentler, crossing a steep, scrubby slope with cliffs above and the barranco below, mostly hacked from a conglomerate ledge. Pass a complex of small caves and turn a corner at

Some of the more basic cave houses at Acusa Seca, before the rugged path round the cliffs

a plaque for **Cruz de la Esquina**, around 800m (2625ft). There is a sudden view of **Acusa Verde** and its fertile fields, with Altavista high above, and the barranco dropping to La Aldea. The path drops and rises across a rugged slope, flanked by prickly pears, marked by a line of cairns.

Join a track and follow it to a road, turning right uphill to pass fine cave houses. The road climbs and winds on scrubby slopes, with almond trees, and there are lots of hairpin bends on the way up to **Vega de Acusa** and the church of La Candelaria. Follow the road onwards, overlooking the **Presa de la Candelaria**. Turn right at a junction, then either turn left to climb back to Artenara, or follow the road back to the car park near Acusa Seca.

LA ALDEA

Cultivation under wraps at La Aldea, as seen from the lower slopes of Montaña del Viso (Walk 19)

The town of La Aldea is also known as San Nicolás de Tolentino. It lies in a fertile valley far removed from other centres of population on Gran Canaria. Its huddled, whitewashed buildings are completely surrounded by fields and terraces covered in cultivation tents. Despite its remoteness, the town has good bus services; it can also be reached from distant Artenara by walkers willing to walk a long way through increasingly arid landscapes.

One long but fairly easy approach involves following the Pista de Tirma – a convoluted forest road linking with a bus service. A more rugged upland approach crosses the forested mountain Altavista, then descends through arid, scrub-covered areas to reach La Aldea.

One walk from La Aldea climbs onto rugged, arid slopes to link with the Pista de Tirma, then descends to the little settlement of El Risco, where a bus can be caught back to town. One fairly popular walk starts near La Aldea, and crosses rugged mountain gaps and deep barrancos to reach Güigüí and Tasártico, where a pick-up needs to be arranged at the finish. The steep and rocky mountain of Viso looks unassailable from La Aldea, but there are breaches in its cliffs that walkers can exploit, and it is a remarkable viewpoint.

At the time of writing, the PR GC routes in La Aldea have not yet been numbered. They are currently designated on signposts as 'PR GC XXX'.

WALK 15
Pista de Tirma

Start	Casa Forestal de Tirma
Finish	Andén Verde
Distance	19km (12 miles)
Total Ascent	150m (490ft)
Total Descent	800m (2625ft)
Time	5hrs
Terrain	A clear and obvious forest road, mostly downhill, with a few gentle uphill stretches, that can be covered quite quickly.
Refreshments	None.
Transport	Taxi from Artenara to Casa Forestal de Tirma. Occasional buses from Andén Verde link La Aldea and Agaete.

The Pista de Tirma is a forest road, offering a long, easy walk, popular with cyclists too. It runs mostly down through a remote forested area of Gran Canaria. A taxi is needed to reach the Finca de Tirma, and while buses can be caught at the finish, study the timetable carefully and make sure the driver sees you!

The remote house of **Casa Forestal de Tirma** stands at 1184m (3885ft), beside the road running from Artenara to Tamadaba. Either reach it by taxi, or follow Walk 42 in reverse from Artenara. Leave the road and pass gate pillars to reach the house, swinging left to continue. The forest road is very bendy as it descends pine-covered slopes, so views are seen from all possible angles. The dirt road has been cut from rock in places and there are always whitewashed stones along its outside edge. As the road turns round the head of the **Barranco del Vaquero** it passes a dry waterfall, then it turns a prominent corner and drifts gently down around another barranco.

There are sweeping zigzags down to a junction at **El Vaquero**. A house and reservoir lie down to the right,

so keep left and rise gently. Turn round another barranco, then consider a short detour along a spur track onto a promontory at **Cruz de La Virgen**, around 880m (2885ft), where there is a fine view down to El Risco. However, continue along the forest road, gently downhill, then down interminable zigzags on a steep slope. The **Barranco Hoya del Laurel** is seen from every conceivable vantage point.

Cross the deep, steep-sided, rocky barranco, where water is drawn off just above a bridge. Pines are sparse on the lower slopes and the dirt road runs gently downhill, winding in and out of little valleys.

Walkers approach the Casa Forestal de Tirma at the start of the long, winding, forested Pista de Tirma

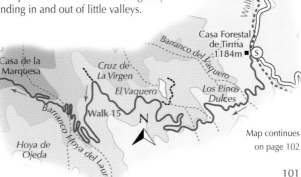

Map continues on page 102

101

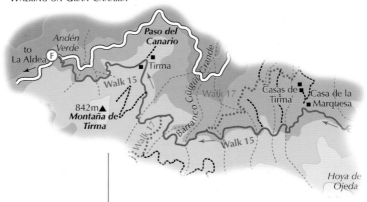

To the right is a track linking with Walk 17, offering a descent to El Risco.

Looking down on the little reservoir of Presa de Tirma, couched in a forested hollow

There is another zigzag, then the track approaches **Casa de la Marquesa**, at 560m (1835ft). ◄ Keep left as signposted for Andén Verde, up the bendy forest road, often with a water pipe alongside. The slopes have been reforested and also bear cistus. Keep rising, noting pastel shades around the **Barranco Güigüí Grande**. Another track climbs left, used by Walk 17 from La Aldea, so stay on the forest road and continue round one last big, barren barranco.

Pass a house at **Tirma**, where there are huge prickly pears, and a wonderful variety of trees, shrubs and flowers. Pass a barrier and note a rocky knoll covered in cardón. The dirt road bends sharp left and runs downhill with a view of rocky ridges falling steeply seawards. Puerto de las Nieves can be seen along the coast, and a little shrine is seen tucked into the mountainside on the left. The track finally zigzags down to a sign for Finca de Tirma, and there is a bus shelter beside the road at **Andén Verde**, at 550m (1805ft). Make sure that the bus driver sees you on this remote and very bendy road!

WALK 16

Altavista to La Aldea

Start	Degollada del Sargento
Finish	La Aldea
Distance	20km (12½ miles)
Total Ascent	470m (1540ft)
Total Descent	1570m (5150ft)
Time	7hrs
Terrain	Good paths and tracks most of the time, sometimes steep and rugged. Forested slopes give way to increasingly scrubby or barren slopes, with a long descent towards the end.
Refreshments	Plenty of choice in La Aldea.
Transport	Taxi from Artenara to Degollada del Sargento. Regular daily buses link La Aldea with Gáldar, Agaete and Mógan.

Altavista is a splendid viewpoint in a remote, forested part of Gran Canaria. A there-and-back walk is possible from Degollada del Sargento, but a finer walk leads beyond the summit and forest, across arid scrubland, down steep, rugged, barren slopes to the agricultural town of La Aldea.

Route uses PR GC XXX.

Start from a mirador and parking space at **Degollada del Sargento**, around 1160m (3805ft), between Artenara and Tamadaba. Either reach it by taxi, or follow Walk 42 in reverse from Artenara. There are views of Moriscos, Pico de las Nieves, Roque Nublo, Roque Bentayga, Inagua and Vega de Acusa. There is a map-board, and a well-worn path climbs among pines and a few tagasaste, with a ground cover of cistus and rock-rose. Reach a sign-posted junction (right is for Tamadaba) and keep left for Altavista, passing **Cruz de María**.

Keep climbing and the path becomes gentle among pines and rock-rose, crossing a crest from side to side. There is a prominent descent to a rocky gap where there are good views on both sides, stretching to the right as far as El Teide and Tenerife. The path rises and falls, often buttressed or hacked from rock, crossing a steep, rocky, forested slope to another gap. There is a stony climb, becoming easier, followed by a traverse round **Risco Alto**. There is a deeper and more rugged gap, where the path winds down to an abrupt rocky edge with views on both sided. Climb the other side to reach a junction.

The view from Altavista to distant La Aldea, and clearly there is no direct route for walkers!

Keep left and zigzag up a forested slope, which becomes increasingly steep and rocky, then the path slices across the slope, rising and falling gently, before dropping past an overhanging outcrop to a rocky gap. Climb again, passing below a trig point at 1376m (4514ft) on **Altavista**, reaching a cliff edge with sudden and extensive views. La Aldea and its cultivation tents can be seen far ahead, but cannot be approached directly. Retrace steps down the zigzags and turn left at the junction.

The author above Meseta de Carreños, with Altavista rising beyond

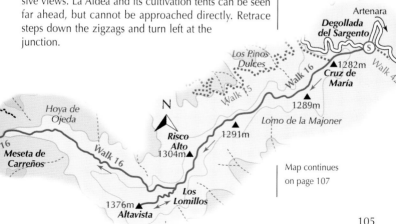

Map continues on page 107

105

The path is stone-paved as it rises across the northern slopes of Altavista, becoming gentler and more even underfoot. It then winds downhill between cliffs, rough and stony, in a shaded hollow. There are pines,

La Pimien

Fuente Salado

Montaña Cueva del Humo

Fuente Blanca

Walk 17

Walk 16

Morro de los Pinos

Walk 16

Greenhouses

La Aldea

F

a few tagasaste, broom, cistus and asphodel. At a fork, keep right to descend the broader of two paths, later generally rising across a rocky slope, continuing easily across a slope of pines. Watch for a pinnacle of rock holding a huge boulder wedged against a cliff. The path rises onto a rocky, arid crest above **Hoya de Ojeda** and **Meseta de Carreños**, with fewer pines and more cistus and tabaibal, with a view ahead to La Aldea.

Follow the path downhill, where it becomes narrow and vague in places among cistus and tabaibal, but is marked with small cairns on rocky slopes. There is a prominent boulder perched on a rocky ridge, then a rise, with El Teide in view all the time. The path winds tightly – worn, stony and crumbling – rising to traverse the right-hand side of a rounded hill bearing a solitary pine. Continue down along the crest, then note a path falling to the left and rising to the right, towards pines. Go down the path on the left, rough and stony, sometimes rocky, and note how the scrub becomes richer. There is

still cistus and tabaibal, but also verode and white tajinaste.

The path descends to a track near a hut beside **Montaña Cueva del Humo**. Either cross the track and follow an old path down a bit, then up to a slight gap, or just turn right and follow the track up to the gap. The path descends as a stony groove through scrub, crossing a track twice and passing close to a ramshackle hut in a small clump of trees. Walk down the path, past a couple of pine trees, crossing a streambed among spiky rushes at **Fuente Salado**. The path continues, rising and falling on scrubby, stony slopes, while a barranco falls away sharply to the left. An abrupt edge is suddenly reached, around 760m (2495ft), overlooking La Aldea.

A winding, stone-paved path leads down a rocky ramp, then a winding, stony path runs down through scrub, reaching a track and a three-way signpost on **Morro de los Pinos**. ▶ Turn left down a rough and stony track, signposted for La Aldea. Watch for a short-cut marked by cairns, roughly parallel to a broken pipeline. Follow the zigzag track further downhill, which has been severed by little gullies and storm damage. Again, watch for little cairns that reveal narrow paths short-cutting some bends. Do not be drawn off-route towards greenhouses.

Land in a valley and turn left to follow a track, rising a little, then running downhill, stone-paved, to a house. A concrete road continues downhill, then keep left along a tarmac road. This becomes a dirt road crossing two riverbeds. A tarmac road continues into **La Aldea**, around 60m (195ft). Turn right to aim for the twin towers of a church on a plaza. The town is also known as San Nicolás de Tolentino (hotel, pensión, shops, bar/restaurants, banks with ATMs, post office, buses and taxis).

Walk 17 climbs to the right, for El Risco.

WALK 17
La Aldea to El Risco

Start	La Aldea
Finish	El Risco
Distance	15km (9½ miles)
Total Ascent/Descent	800m (2625ft)
Time	5hrs
Terrain	Some good farm and forest tracks, but also some rugged paths on steep, stony or rocky slopes.
Refreshments	Plenty of choice in La Aldea. Bar at El Risco.
Transport	Occasional daily buses link La Aldea and El Risco with Agaete and Galdár.

Leaving La Aldea, a long climb up rugged, arid slopes is followed by a fine traverse across a cliff face to a remote goat farm. Forest tracks and paths lead to the Casas de Tirma, from where a steep and rugged path drops to El Risco. This route links with two other linear routes – Walk 15 and Walk 16.

Route uses PR GC XXX.

Start at the church and plaza in **La Aldea**, around 60m (195ft), walking along a road and a pedestrianised street, Calle General Franco. This runs straight, then bends right as it rises gently to a junction at El Corral. Turn left down Calle Sargento Provisional, which quickly leaves town and becomes a dirt road crossing two riverbeds. It becomes tarmac again, then head straight up a crumbling concrete road, passing a signpost for El Risco and Tirma. Climb steeply past the last houses, and go up a short, steep, stone-paved path. Cross a rise and head gently down into a valley. Before the broad path rises again towards **greenhouses**, turn right across a streambed to find an old, winding, stony groove of a path.

Follow the path up to an old track and keep climbing, flanked by two old water channels. Before the track levels out, step up to the left onto another track. Cross it and follow the old path further uphill, crossing another track.

Climb again and cross the track again. Wind further uphill, cross the track yet again, noting a concrete hut down to the right. Climb to a higher part of the track and turn right to follow it, turning left round a bend. Keep climbing and the gradient eases for a while, then climb steeply again. Note a fractured water pipe, which can be followed straight up a stony slope covered in tabaibal, avoiding bends. Rejoin the track and walk up to a three-way signpost, around 570m (1870ft), at **Morro de los Pinos**. ▸

Turn left up the track, signposted for El Risco and Tirma, to a concrete hut. A stony path climbs past monstrous boulders, heading towards cliffs. Note a buried pipeline peeping through, except where the path takes a different course. The path and pipeline exploit soft cream and green coloured layers, with sheer cliffs above and below. The path is broad and there is little sense of exposure. Turn a corner at **Fuente Blanco** and the path narrows on a steep, rocky and well-vegetated slope. The most notable plants are tall, yellow umbellifers called *cañalejas*.

Follow the path, as the pipeline often runs at a higher level. Views across a broad barranco stretch to El Teide and Tenerife. Turn another corner to spot a goat farm tucked into a mountainside hollow at **Cuevas Negras**. Walk down a slope of bare rock and pass below little terraces in a barranco. Climb a rocky ramp and keep well below the buildings, watching for the line of the path on a goat-grazed slope of tabaibal and verode. Red and white concrete posts help on

Walk 16 heads right for Altavista.

Map continues on page 110

109

The path exploits a little terrace half-way up the cliff face to reach Fuente Blanco

the way to a signpost, cairn and cross on a gap around 730m (2395ft).

Walk ahead as signposted for El Risco and Tirma, with views of Tamadaba and Risco Faneque. Go down a track, then either go left down an indistinct path marked by tiny cairns on a slope of cistus and tabaibal, or continue up the track, keep left at junctions, heading down to a broad forest road. Either way, turn right to follow the forest road, which is flanked by whitewashed stones. ◄ The bendy dirt road runs

Left is Walk 15 to Andén Verde.

110

gently downhill, with pines above and scrub below, turning round the **Barranco Güigüi Grande**, around 600m (1970ft).

On one right-hand bend, watch for a couple of little cairns on the left. Walk this way a few paces then turn right along an old path. ▶ Zigzag downhill and turn round a rocky barranco, climbing from it among cistus and tabaibal. The path enjoys fine views, crosses another streambed and rises along a rocky edge. A falling traverse along the rocky edge leads to a straggly fence and track. Walk gently down the track, which later rises with palms alongside below the attractive **Casas de Tirma**. Turn left down a track signposted 'Camino Real', reaching a promontory overlooking deeply-cut barrancos.

The path slips down to the right, clear and stony. Follow it, but note that an unseen cliff later prevents a direct descent, so the path heads right and zigzags to avoid it. Continue down one side or the other of the broken rocky crest above **Charco Hondo**. When houses are reached, follow an access road to a main road and turn right to cross the Barranco del Risco. Finish at the Bar Perdomo in **El Risco**, where there are bus stops.

The forest road continues to Casa Forestal de Tirma as Walk 15.

A cross and cairn on a rugged little gap near the goat farm of Cuevas Negras

WALK 18
Albercón, Güigüí and Tasártico

Start	Albercón
Finish	Tasártico
Distance	15km (9½ miles)
Total Ascent	1400m (4595ft)
Total Descent	1250m (4100ft)
Time	6hrs
Terrain	Mostly rugged, steep and stony paths, over high passes and across deep barrancos, on steep, rocky, arid mountains.
Refreshments	None.
Transport	Regular daily buses serve Albercón from La Aldea, Agaete and Gáldar. Taxi needs to be arranged from Tasártico.

This route crosses arid mountains using convoluted mule paths, with an optional beach walk halfway. A couple of habitations in the barrancos cling to existence by exploiting little trickles of water. The spelling of 'Güigüí' varies throughout this walk, and all forms are noted, as there is no consensus.

Route uses PR GC XXX.

Start in the little village of **Albercón**, around 50m (165ft). A signpost points up the Calle Subida Cuermeja, for 'Guyguy'. Climb past houses beside a bouldery barranco. There are views of Altavista and Inagua, with Roque Bentayga framed between them. The road finally swings left, but leave it as signposted 'Guyguy', up a path between stone-built **reservoirs**.

The path is stony, rocky or stone-paved as it winds uphill, and the scrub alongside is remarkably mixed, thorny and flowery, with prominent clumps of cardón. Dip to cross a little side-valley, then further uphill, stay on the clearest path in and out of a couple more side-valleys, passing a ruin. Keep left to climb above an inhabited house, as signposted 'Guguy'.

Keep winding and climbing, then there are level traverses around a couple of side-valleys. The path climbs

A path climbs past a cliff face to the gap of Degollada del Peñón Bermejo

steep and rugged, and side to side across a barranco bed, as if heading for cliffs. However, there is suddenly a gentle traverse along a ledge to the rocky gap of **Degollada del Peñón Bermejo**, at 672m (2205ft). Look back to La Aldea and Tamadaba, and across the other side to see barrancos dropping seawards. El Teide and Tenerife are in view.

Map continues on page 114

The path traverses and climbs further along a rocky ledge on a steep and rugged mountainside. A big **boulder** is painted 'Degoya de Güígüí Chico', and looking ahead, rocky ridges and deep barrancos are seen. The path drops sharply, sometimes on rock, or stone-paved, or stone-strewn, winding down slopes of bushy tabaibal, with some verode, spiky aulaga and tall cardón further down. Palms trees can be seen deep in the barranco and the path winds down to them. Pass cultivated plots, then a tangle of palms and canes in

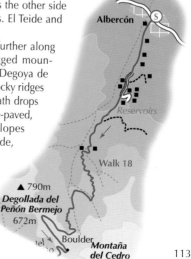

Albercón

Reservoirs

Walk 18

▲ 790m
Degollada del Peñón Bermejo
672m

Boulder

Montaña del Cedro

113

the **Barranco Güigüí Chico**, as the path rises towards a little house.

Keep right along a narrow path, joining a path leaving the house. Continue across the scrub-covered slopes of the barranco on a rising traverse that is surprisingly even. Bend round the slopes and pass tabaibal, verode and cardón. Climb to a rocky notch, where there is a view of El Teide across the sea. Look down the other side to see old terraces deep in the barranco, as well as dramatic mountains and ridges beyond. The path makes an easy traverse, becoming quite rugged as it drops steeply. Pass particularly tall, stout and tangled tabaibal and clumps of cardón.

Cross the bed of the **Barranco Güigüí Grande** among old terraces, palms and boulders, below 200m (655ft). Follow the path from ruin to ruin, crossing the barranco bed again, reaching a three-way signpost. There is an option to walk down to a beach, and, if the tide permits, to another beach, otherwise turn left as signposted for Tasártico, and cross the bed of the barranco again.

Extension to Playa de Güigüí

This walk can be extended by 3km (2 miles) to take in the sandy Playa de Güigüí, if the tide permits. Walk down the path signposted 'Playa de Guguy' and later cross the bed of the barranco. Painted arrows also assist with route-finding. Keep away from huts at **El Puerto** and

▲790m
Degollada del Peñón Bermejo
672m
Barranco del Peñón Bermejo
Boulder
Montaña del Cedro
Barranco Güigüí Chico
Farm
N
Playa de Güigüí
Walk 18
Barranco Güigüí Grande
El Puerto
Degollada de Aguas Sabinas
La Aldea
Tasártico
▲736m
Montaña de Aguas Sabinas
Walk 18
Barranco de Tasártico

push through cane thickets in the bed of the barranco, to find a rocky ramp down to a cobble beach. Turn right and walk to **Playa de Güigüí**, retracing steps to the three-way signpost.

A ruined farmstead is passed, deep in the Barranco Güigüí Grande

The path for Tasártico is indistinct after it crosses the bed of the Barranco Güigüí Grande, so watch carefully as it winds up past scrub and crosses another barranco bed. Continue up beside the bed, then follow the bed itself a short way, looking for an exit on the right. The path climbs to a crest, swinging left for a rising traverse, joining another path rising from El Puerto. Cross the bed of another barranco and climb towards old telegraph poles.

The poles can be seen crossing a V-shaped gap in the mountains, which the path also crosses, though it takes a much longer zigzag course. The path climbs steep and rocky slopes, picking out breaches in cliffs and traversing a long and exciting ledge. A final set of zigzags climb to the gap and a rocky notch, **Degollada de Aguas Sabinas**, at almost 600m (1970ft). Take a last look back, spotting El Teide out to sea, then drop down the other side.

The walk can be extended down to the sea, and, if tides allow, to Playa de Güigüí

The path winds downhill, steep and stone-strewn, with a view of a farm and cultivated area. The path drifts well to the right of the barranco, then further down it switches to the left of the barranco. The final stretch is a more even gravel path, swinging left and winding down to a dirt road and signpost in the **Barranco de Tasártico**. Turn left and follow the dirt road uphill, keeping right of most buildings in **Tasártico**, joining a tarmac road. ▸

A taxi needs to be arranged to leave the village.

WALK 19
Montaña del Viso and La Aldea

Start	Degollada de La Aldea
Finish	La Aldea
Distance	12km (7½ miles)
Total Ascent	400m (1310ft)
Total Descent	1000m (3280ft)
Time	5hrs
Terrain	Mostly rugged paths, narrow and exposed on the ascent, then steep and rocky on the descent, ending with easy road-walking.
Refreshments	Plenty of choice in La Aldea.
Transport	Occasional daily buses link La Aldea with the Degollada de La Aldea.

Montaña del Viso, or just plain Viso, towers above La Aldea and a direct ascent looks impossible. This route starts from the Degollada de la Aldea, offering an easier, but exposed approach to the summit. Careful attention to route-finding is needed on the steep and rocky descent.

Start on the **Degollada de La Aldea**, at a road junction with bus stops, around 670m (2200ft). There is a signpost for Montaña del Viso, and a stony path climbs and crosses a gritty crest. Monstrous tiered cliffs rise above, with pines along the skyline, hiding the summit of Inagua. The

Route uses PR GC XXX.

path rises gently across a steep and well-vegetated slope, then there is a sudden, hands-on scramble up to a vegetated ledge with sheer cliffs above and below. Although the path is well trodden, it is unsuitable for anyone suffering vertigo.

The path runs beneath a big pine and there are a few smaller pines on the slope. The ledge is like a narrow stone pavement, hammered out of rock. There is a feeling of height being gained, but this is an illusion, as it is actually the valley below falling! Take care where the cliff nudges walkers to the edge of the path. Pass a straggly fence and the traverse soon ends. A sudden climb leads between house-sized boulders, where small boulders have been piled into crude steps. Scramble up past dense vegetation. Some of the boulders stand as **pinnacles** and the path passes between them.

Ahead, gentler slopes bear sparse pines and the path is stony. A mass of rock rises to the right and it is important to watch for a right turn marked by small cairns. Step up easily on rock to a signpost on a broad crest, over 1000m (3280ft). Turn left as indicated for La Aldea. The crest has a lot of bare rock, but a slight path runs almost level,

The trig point on the summit of Montaña del Viso, looking down on cultivated slopes

passing
cistus and
a few short
pines. A
track crosses
the crest, and
it could be fol-
lowed down to
the left to save time,
but this omits a fine
viewpoint.

Stay on the broad, rocky,
gently undulating crest, picking a way past cistus and tabaibal,
until a rocky hump can be climbed
to reach a trig point on **Montaña del Viso**, at
997m (3271ft). Views stretch down to La Aldea and
the coast, past Tirma, Risco Faneque, Tamadaba and
Altavista to Artenara. Peaks include Moriscos, Roque
Bentayga, Roque Nublo, Pico de las Nieves and nearby
Inagua. Looking towards Güigüí, El Teide and Tenerife are
seen far beyond. Retrace steps to the track and turn right
to follow it. Avoid the temptation to short-cut west from
Viso to the track, as it is too dangerous.

The track descends easily past a few tall pines and
several younger ones, reaching a **turning space**.
Continue straight down a rugged path, often in
a groove flanked by cistus and tabaibal, passing
the last few little pines. The path aligns itself to
a crest, but quickly turns right between a couple
of boulders and winds down through worn, stony
grooves to a bright bald patch, where the rock features peculiar shades, near **Lomo del Arrastradero**.

Keep right and watch for small, reddish cairns across
the bright, crumbling expanse of rock. The cairns later
swing left to reveal a rugged path winding down what is
essentially a landslide of the bright rock, broken and jumbled. Eventually, the path shifts onto red rock, more vegetated, with clumps of tabaibal and tajinaste. La Aldea can
be seen, but isn't reached for some time. The path winds

119

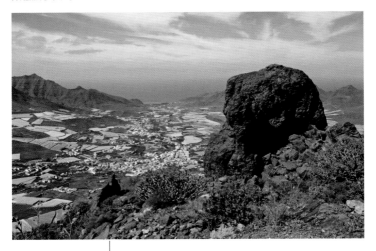

View of La Aldea and its surrounding cultivated slopes, on the descent from Montaña del Viso

down past a prominent large red boulder and passes a few almond trees. Any remaining stone paving is lumpy and awkward, and most of the time the path runs through a stony groove among increasingly rampant scrub.

A long, falling traverse runs below a cliff full of caves, where the path exploits crumbling layers of rock. Keep winding down, passing right of a reservoir to land on a track. Cross over to follow the path further downhill. Cross and re-cross a pipe, passing a water store and a shed. The path becomes flanked by walls and prickly pears, later swinging right to cross a little valley to reach a narrow road and signpost.

Turn left down the road, between cultivation tents. When the tarmac turns right, follow it, then turn left downhill. Turn right down past the **Coagrisan** depot and a cactus garden. Turn left over a bridge spanning a river-bed, along the road, turning right along Calle Monteverde into **La Aldea**. Keep right of a tiny, shaded park at a road junction, and walk down Calle General Franco, swinging left at a junction at El Corral. Continue along a pedestrianised street and aim for the twin towers of the church, around 60m (195ft). ◄

For facilities in La Aldea, see the end of Walk 16.

MOGÁN AND LAS PRESAS

The Presa de Soria is one of three large reservoirs in this part of Gran Canaria (Walk 24)

The mountain road linking Ayacata, El Aserrador and Tejeda has a reasonable bus service and allows high-level starting points for walks. One of these is almost a circuit, linking with the bus at either end, taking in the tiny villages of El Toscón, El Carrizal, El Manatial, El Chorillo and El Espinillo. Another circuit takes in a splendid, sparsely forested mountain ridge, before descending to the mountain village of El Juncal.

The road between the low-lying village of Mogán and the mountain village of Ayacata used to be one of the worst on Gran Canaria – a rutted and boulder-strewn dirt track capable of wrecking a car. Now it is a splendid scenic road allowing some wonderful walks to be reached, including a forested circuit above the reservoir of Presa de las Niñas. There is also access a mountain-climb on Montaña de Tauro, followed by a long and gradual descent, then a sudden and very steep descent to Mogán.

The Camino de las Presas is a long route linking three large reservoirs. These prove to be quite attractive when full, but less so when they run low, revealing sterile stony shores. This walk works best if a pickup can be arranged, otherwise it is a very long route if stretched to link with bus services.

121

WALK 20
El Aserrador and El Carrizal

Start	El Aserrador
Finish	Casas de la Umbria
Distance	15km (9½ miles)
Total Ascent	950m (3115ft)
Total Descent	1260m (4135ft)
Time	5hrs
Terrain	Some easy roads and tracks linking villages, but also some rugged paths in barrancos or across steep slopes.
Refreshments	None.
Transport	Occasional daily buses serve Degollada del Aserrador and Casas de la Umbria from Tejeda, Ayacata, San Bartolomé and Maspalomas.

This walk goes from one little village to another, with views of surrounding mountains, and sometimes penetrates deep into barrancos. Towards the end, the route passes close to the towering Roque Bentayga – a sacred Guanche ritual site pock-marked with caves.

Route uses PR GC 80.

Start at a road junction at **El Aserrador**, around 1350m (4430ft). Take the road signposted for El Carrizal and the PR GC 80. Go down the road and keep straight ahead as signposted for El Carrizal. The road levels out on a gap and keeps left of a rocky mountain overlooking the **Barranco del Juncal**. Rise through a rock cutting then note a signposted path on the left, with a view to the village of El Toscón, with Altavista to the right, El Teide and Tenerife far beyond, and La Aldea near the coast.

The path zigzags down and is stone-paved past almond trees. As the almonds peter out, the path is boulder-paved or crosses bare rock, and the bed of the **Barranco del Toscón** is also bare rock. Climb fairly easily, rising and falling along a cliff path flanked by aloes. Rise to a road and signpost and continue straight ahead. The

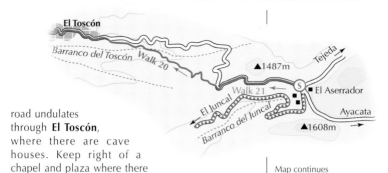

road undulates through **El Toscón**, where there are cave houses. Keep right of a chapel and plaza where there is another view of distant El Teide.

Map continues on page 124

Go down the winding road, past more houses, reaching a rocky gap where there is a fine view of **Roque Palmés**. Either go down the bendy road below a goat farm, or leave the road on the gap and follow a path tracing a stone-covered water pipe. If the latter is chosen, drop to a junction between a road bend and a track. Either way, a signpost for the PR GC 80 points down a path into the **Barranco del Carrizal**.

The path is part concrete and part stone-paved, then quite rugged down into the barranco. Cross the rocky

An avalanche of white houses makes up the little village of El Carrizal

123

Map continues
on page 126

bed, not a footbridge that serves a potato patch. Don't climb to the road, but follow the path between the streambed and road, down through the barranco on scrubby slopes of verode and tajinaste. Cross the streambed again and follow a delightful path across slopes of almonds, looking ahead to white houses. Cross back to the scrubbier side of the barranco and follow a rugged path towards houses. Wind steeply downhill from the first house to a road and signpost, around 750m (2460ft).

Turn right up the road to a junction in **El Carrizal**, and turn right up the road signposted for El Toscón. Walk up to another road junction and turn left as signposted for El Chorillo, walking to a house at the end of the tarmac. A path signposted up to the right makes a rising traverse, climbing and zigzagging round a steep and scrubby slope. Pass aloes, prickly pears, tabaibal, verode, tajinaste and broom, overlooking a reservoir, Inagua, El Teide and Altavista.

Cross a crest and turn sharp right downhill a little. A splendid, gentle, rising traverse follows a path hacked from a weak layer of rock, around 800m (2625ft), sometimes with overhangs above, while steep, scrubby slopes drop to a deep barranco. ◄ Old telegraph poles stand beside the path, and a cave full of water is passed. The slope eases, losing its cliffs, but remains steep and scrubby. The descent mostly follows a groove, either on bare rock, or boulder paving, with views across the barranco. The last part of the path rises to a signpost beside a concrete road.

Views stretch from Altavista and Vega de Acusa to Brezos, Artenara, Moriscos and Roque Bentayga.

Turn left down the road, but don't go down hairpin bends. Instead, head right as signposted, down a concrete path through **El Manantial**. Turn left and right down steps between buildings and land on a tarmac road. Walk down the bendy road with views of Roque Bentayga and Roque Nublo on the skyline, then cross the bed of the **Barranco del Chorillo**, where there might be a river in cane thickets, around 570m (1870ft).

Walk up the road to a signpost and turn sharp right up a stone-paved ramp. A gently rising terrace path crosses a couple of streambeds, continuing as a track past cultivated plots. A signpost indicates a left turn up a steep concrete road, but on the way up, turn right up concrete steps, winding between buildings to reach the shaded Plaza La Milagrosa and a chapel in **El Chorillo**. Watch for a signpost and follow a stone-paved path up from the plaza, later levelling out and dropping to leave the village.

A splendid and easy path cuts across a steep slope between El Carrizal and El Manantial

125

The Roque Bentayga looms over El Chorillo, and was once sacred to the Guanches

A short detour can include the Mirador de La Virgen.

A rough and stony path drops into a barranco. Zigzag up a slope of mixed scrub, levelling out among dense scrub where there is a solitary building with a pine tree alongside. The path follows the bed of the barranco a short way, with Roque Bentayga towering above. Leave the bed at a few almond trees, winding and climbing past dense scrub, occasional tagasaste and aloes on a steep and rocky slope. Reach a ridge and continue up it, flanked by mixed scrub. The path leads to a road-end turning space, around 900m (2950ft) at **El Espinillo**. ◄

Walk up the road to leave the village, watching for a signpost pointing left. A stone-paved and stony path

winds up a slope of tabaibal, verode and broom, dotted with aloes. Pass a huge boulder and level out on a crest facing Roque Bentayga, then climb to a road. Cross as signposted and continue climbing, passing a few almond trees among the scrub. Walk over a crest and gently down a bit, then up to a road and signpost. ▸

Turn right, gently down the road to a junction. Turn right up a road, enjoying views of the surrounding mountains. Walk through a cutting and down to a junction at **Casas de la Umbria**, around 1160m (3805ft), for bus services.

Turn left up the road to visit the Centro de Interpretación del Bentayga, which explains how the Roque Bentayga was sacred to the original Guanche inhabitants of Gran Canaria.

WALK 21
El Aserrador and El Juncal

Start/Finish	El Aserrador
Distance	13km (8 miles)
Total Ascent/Descent	710m (2330ft)
Time	4hrs
Terrain	A rugged mountain ridge is followed by an easy forest road into a valley, followed by a road-walk.
Refreshments	None.
Transport	Occasional daily buses serve Degollada del Aserrador from Tejeda, Ayacata, San Bartolomé and Maspalomas.

The highlight of this walk is an attractive rocky crest, blessed with a good path and occasional views. The rest of the walk is simply down a forest road and up a tarmac road. However, strong walkers could continue along Walk 22 and link with Walk 23, descending towards Mogán to finish.

Start at a road junction at **El Aserrador**, around 1350m (4430ft). Take the road signposted for El Carrizal, but quickly turn left as signposted down a road for El Juncal. Turn round the head of the **Barranco del Juncal** on slopes of trees, bushy scrub and boulders. The road turns right, then

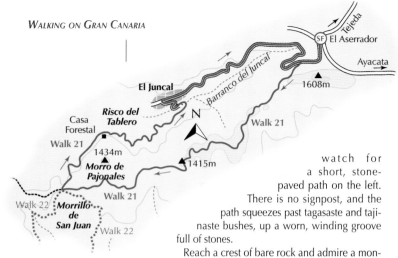

watch for a short, stone-paved path on the left. There is no signpost, and the path squeezes past tagasaste and tajinaste bushes, up a worn, winding groove full of stones.

The path descends from Morro de Pajonales to a forested gap crossed by a dirt road

Reach a crest of bare rock and admire a monstrous tower of rock. The path continues past a variety of scrub to a gap. The ridge ahead is very rough and rocky, but the path outflanks every difficulty, rising and falling, winding and zigzagging from gap to gap, avoiding rocky peaks over 1400m (4595ft). Much of the way is among pines, where views come and go, taking in

El Juncal, Altavista, Montaña de Tauro, Maspalomas and distant El Teide on Tenerife. The roller-coaster path eventually passes **Morro de Pajonales** and becomes stone-paved, with stone steps, as it drops to a forest road on a gap over 1200m (3940ft). ▶

Walk 22 joins here.

Turn right to follow the bendy forest road, gently up and down, passing the **Casa Forestal**, or forestry house. Catch a glimpse of El Teide and continue down the bendy dirt road to the bed of the **Barranco del Juncal**, around 1100m (3610ft). A tarmac road zigzags up into the little village of **El Juncal**. Turn right to follow the road up alongside the barranco, counting off three kilometre markers on the way back up to **El Aserrador**.

WALK 22
Presa de las Niñas and Morrillo de San Juan

Start/Finish	Cruce de la Data
Distance	10km (6¼ miles)
Total Ascent/Descent	305m (1000ft)
Time	3hrs
Terrain	A clear path climbs a forested slope, and a forest road is used to descend afterwards, ending with an easy road-walk.
Refreshments	None.
Transport	None.

This short circular walk lies in a forested area remote from bus routes. The winding mountain road from Mogán to Cruz de San Antonio used to be dreadful, but it has been completely rebuilt and offers a splendid scenic approach for walkers who have their own vehicles.

Cruce de la Data is a road and track junction, around 950m (3115ft), beside a solitary farm between Mogán and Ayacata. It is a long way from bus services and too far to

A view of the whole of the Presa de las Niñas, seen while descending a forest road

consider hiring an expensive taxi for the day, so walkers with their own transport have the advantage. A path climbs northwards from the junction, straight up a slope of pine trees, flanked by a low drystone wall. The path levels out with a view of a reservoir – Presa de las Niñas.

Keep climbing without the benefit of views, or the low stone wall, and the ground becomes rocky. Cross a crest and descend a while to cross a streambed. Climb again, then dip to cross another stream-bed. Climb yet again on

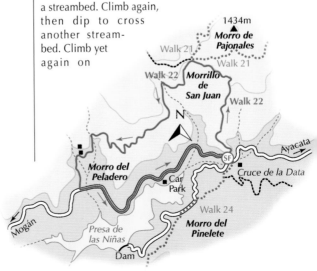

Morrillo de San Juan, and stone-paved steps lead up to a forest road on a gap over 1200m (3940ft). ▸

Walk 21 joins here.

Turn left along the dirt road, following its very bendy course generally downhill, with only a couple of gentle ascents. The slopes are covered in pines and little else, while occasional views reveal the reservoir below, as well as Montaña de Tauro. Pass below some buildings, and the forest road eventually joins a tarmac road, around 950m (3115ft), at **Morro del Peladero**. ▸

Turn right to follow the road 2km (1¼ miles) to Cruz de San Antonio to reach the start of Walk 23.

Turn left to follow the road, heading towards the reservoir of **Presa de las Niñas**. Pass a car park and continue beyond the head of the reservoir to follow the road back to **Cruce de la Data**.

WALK 23
Cruz de San Antonio to Las Casillas

Start	Cruz de San Antonio
Finish	Las Casillas, Mógan
Distance	13km (8 miles)
Total Ascent	380m (1245ft)
Total Descent	1150m (3775ft)
Time	4hrs
Terrain	Mostly rough and stony paths, sometimes on steep, rocky or forested slopes, and sometimes at gentle gradients. The descent includes cliff-face traverses unsuitable for vertigo sufferers.
Refreshments	Plenty of choice off-route at Mogán.
Transport	Taxi from Mogán to San Antonio. Regular daily buses serve Las Casillas and Mogán from Maspalomas, Puerto de Mogán and La Aldea.

Starting a long way from bus routes, this walk passes Montaña de Tauro and Guirre. There are popular signposted paths, although few nearby habitations. A convoluted path drops from a cliff edge and makes airy traverses before working its way down steep slopes to finish at a fine windmill.

Route uses PR
GC 44, PR GC 45
and PR GC 46.

The road leads
to Soria, linking
with Walk 24.

*After leaving Cruz
de San Antonio, a
path rises through
a gentle valley
near Majada Alta*

Cruz de San Antonio lies around 965m (3165ft), between Mogán and Presa de las Niñas. A track heads east from a large gate, where there is a sign for Cortijo Majada Alta. Although marked 'privada' (private), follow the track past a few pines to find a signpost for the PR GC 44. Go down the bendy track and over a rise, turning right before a fenced enclosure near **Majada Alta**.

Follow a cairned path through grassy and scrubby areas into a gently-sloping valley. Climb easily from it, crossing bare rock, then descend past tabaibal, broom and tajinaste. Turn round a rocky outcrop, with a view into a barranco, then descend mostly on bare rock towards a reservoir, where Montaña de Tauro rises beyond. Keep right of the reservoir and climb to a road, turning left to follow it. ◄

A short, stone-paved path rises on the right of the road, climbing worn and stony through mixed scrub, crossing a crest of bare rock. It rises and falls as it traverses **Montaña Vista de Soria**, clinging to a rocky slope and passing tajinaste bushes. Continue towards pines and bushes and climb a rugged slope. The path levels out on

a bare shoulder and descends gently a short way. Zigzags climb relentlessly on a slope of pines, then the path rises beside a cliff to reach a signposted junction. Left is signposted for Montaña de Tauro, and, while it could be omitted, it is well worth climbing.

So, turn left to follow the path up onto a shoulder covered in rock-rose, where there are substantial drystone enclosures. Swing right to find a scanty path marked by small cairns, climbing a rocky, bouldery slope to the 1214m (3983ft) summit of **Montaña de Tauro**. Views include distant El Teide and Tenerife, nearby mountains around Güigüí, followed by Inagua, Altavista, Moriscos, Roque Nublo and Pico de las Nieves, and finally Maspalomas. Retrace steps to the signposted junction.

The PR GC 45 is signposted for Cortadores and La Solana, climbing steeply among pines and soon levelling out on a shoulder. Follow the path down beside a valley of tall, but sparse pines. The path is occasionally stone-paved, but also rocky and stony. Leave the valley to rise and fall along the rugged path, past cistus and lavender. Drop to a junction beside a **ruin**, around 965m (3165ft), where there are a few more pines. The PR GC 45 is signposted left and right. Turn right and have a look over the cliffs of **Andenes de la Hoya de Almacego** for splendid views.

Map continues on page 134

Map labels:
Ayacata
Cruz de San Antonio S
Presa de las Niñas
Majada Alta
N
Risco Grande
Mogán
Walk 23
Montaña Vista de Soria
Reservoir
El Barranquillo Andrés
Montaña de Tauro 1214m
1003m
Andenes de la Hoya de Almacego
Ruin
Degollada de las Lapas

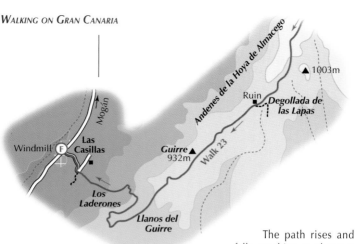

The path rises and falls, reaching another gap with fine views over the edge. Despite the undulations, the overall trend is downhill, occasionally flanked by low walls, passing sparse tall pines. The slopes of **Guirre** bear cistus, tabaibal, lavender and asphodel. Looking ahead, a handful of young pines are seen, and the path passes close to them on **Llanos del Guirre**. A cliff edge is reached around 690m (2265ft), where there is a signpost for the PR GC 46.

A remarkable, tightly zigzagging, stone-paved path is buttressed against the cliff at Los Laderones, with marvellous engineering. It levels out and runs along a ledge with cliffs above and below. A sudden, steep stone buttress leads down to another level traverse with cliffs above and below. Later, zigzag down a steep slope of cistus and tabaibal, cross a scree slope and reach more mixed vegetation. Head straight down a boulder-strewn tongue and later turn right to cross a bouldery streambed to continue downhill. Turn right along a track, then left down a road beside an avocado plantation. Reach the delightful windmill of Molino de Viento at **Las Casillas**, above 200m (655ft), where there are bus services.

A signpost literally points straight over a cliff edge, revealing a remarkable path

WALK 24
Camino de las Presas

Start	Paso Herradura
Finish	Cruce de la Data
Distance	15km (9½ miles)
Total Ascent	485m (1590ft)
Total Descent	760m (2495ft)
Time	5hrs
Terrain	Mostly easy roads and tracks, but also some rough and rocky paths, sometimes crossing steep and rugged slopes.
Refreshments	Bar at Soria.
Transport	Occasional daily buses serve Paso Herradura from Tejeda, Ayacata, San Bartolomé and Maspalomas. Pick-up required at the finish.

The Camino de las Presas is an interesting route that links three large reservoirs. Although there are buses to the start, there are none at the finish, at Cruce de la Data. However, strong walkers can link with parts of Walks 21 and 22 to reach El Juncal, El Aserrador and bus services.

Route uses PR GC 44.

Start at **Paso Herradura**, at a road junction around 1225m (4020ft), between San Bartolomé and Ayacata. Walk down the road signposted for Cercado Araña and Presa de Chira. Enjoy views of high mountains, cliffs, forested slopes and barrancos. A track on the right is signposted for a recreational area, and it immediately forks. Keep left and climb gently to a parking area on a gentle gap beside the **Ermita de Santiago**. There are toilets, notice-boards and stone picnic tables.

Two tracks continue, so take the one down to the left and follow it into a rocky gorge where a surprising number of cultivated plots and curious cave houses are located. Stay on the track all the way down into a streambed then follow a narrow path downstream. The path switches from side to side then runs along the cobbled

Patchy forest and farmland surround the reservoir of Presa de Chira

bed itself. Rise to the left for a splendid view of a reservoir, Presa de Chira, with houses and fields alongside. Pick a way down the rocky path to the foot of a **dry waterfall**, and cross the bed of the barranco.

Step up to a stony path following a rocky ledge at the base of a cliff. There is a water channel, and the path runs below, above, and below it. A fenced enclosure is reached with a view of a small reservoir. Follow a path round a shallow valley, passing left of a concrete building. Keep left to follow a track up a zigzag, head then downhill.

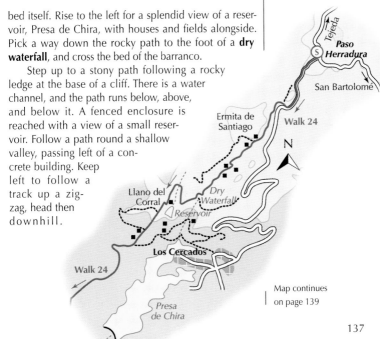

Map continues on page 139

137

The track winds and is partly concrete, passing a large field at **Llano del Corral**. Walk up to a track junction and turn right, either up a stretch of concrete track, or a path short-cutting a bend.

The track rises and falls gently along a broad, rounded crest, which is mostly grassy and stony, with areas of tabaiba, broom and asphodel. Telegraph poles march in a straight line, while the track is bendy. Cross a rise and **Las Casas** is signposted down a track on the right. Don't go that way, but keep left, rising and falling on concrete again, with a view left down to the Presa de Chira dam. Follow the track down and up to another junction. Turn right and keep right down a concrete track onto a stony track at **Las Cuevas**.

Turn left down a rocky and stony path, steep and winding, sometimes with glimpses of a reservoir below. The scrub is remarkably varied, including tajinaste, tabaiba, verode, broom and lavender. When the path splits, keep right down a steep, narrow, rocky and well-worn stony path on the **Risco deí Agujero**. Take care on this descent, catching views of the reservoir. Much further

Walkers descend a steep and rugged path towards the dam of the Presa de Soria

downhill, the path drops into a barranco and goes down it. There are plenty of almond trees among the scrub. As the path comes level with the dam of **Presa de Soria**, around 600m (1970ft), it crosses a bouldery slope.

The reservoir is never full, which is fortunate, as walkers cross what should be its outflow, before climbing metal steps onto the dam. It is a monumental construction, plugging a deep, rocky, steep-sided barranco, with the words 'MAKE A WISH' painted across it! Look far beyond the reservoir to Roque Nublo, and pass a commemorative stone once across the dam. Climb a zigzag road to the little village of **Soria** (bar/restaurant, supermarket and bakery).

Turn right to follow the road up through the village, then wind downhill with views of the reservoir and mountains. There is a bend and a fork leading to a shop, Viveres Sara, but before that point, a chained track climbs on the left. Follow its bendy course uphill until it makes a sudden left turn. At that point, continue straight up a path towards big, bare cliffs. When a rocky streambed is reached, explore upstream a few paces, where there might be a waterfall, pool and shade among enormous boulders.

One boulder is so big that it looks like a cliff and has a cave beneath it.

Continue along the path, which is boulder-paved and winds among cliffs and monstrous boulders. ◄ Keep climbing on bare rock and a stony path, flanked by tajinaste, crossing a shoulder to continue more easily. Head downhill to reach a road and a signpost for the PR GC 44. Turn right and follow the road across a gentle gap, with the reservoir of **Presa de las Niñas** to the left.

When the road rises, turn right up a worn, rocky path on a rugged slope of tabaibal, broom, verode and lavender. The path passes tagasaste, steep, bare rock, then more tagasaste. An easier path links with a track, where a left turn leads to a road at **Cruce de la Data**, around 950m (3115ft), beside a solitary farm between Mogán and Ayacata. This is a long way from bus services, so walkers need to organise a pick-up if finishing here.

It is possible to continue along Walk 22, climbing to Morrillo de San Juan, then continue along Walk 21 down to El Juncal and up to El Aserrador. This links with bus services and adds 9km (5½ miles) to the walk.

TEJEDA AND LA CULATA

The rocky pinnacle of El Fraile, seen here isolated from its larger neighbour, Roque Nublo (Walk 28)

The mountainous heart of Gran Canaria offers some splendid walks, providing that there is good visibility. On days when low cloud brushes the mountains, it can be grey, cold, damp and lacking much scenic merit. On clear days, views are exceptional, taking in deep barrancos, steep terraces, forested slopes, sheer cliffs and remarkable towers of rock piercing the sky – notably Roque Nublo.

Walks in this area are inter-linked, so all kinds of variations are possible. They are mostly well-signposted and waymarked. Old mule paths and forgotten roads can be followed between Cruz de Tejeda and the mountain village of Tejeda. A deep barranco and a high mountain crest can be explored around the villages of Tejeda and La Culata. The imposing tower of Roque Nublo can be approached fairly easily from La Goleta.

Although circular walks are possible around this area, one of the most popular is a linear route, linking with bus services, stretching across the mountains from Cruz Grande to Ayacata. It is also possible to climb the highest mountain on the island, Pico de las Nieves, from El Garañón. However, it is also possible for motorists to drive almost all the way to the summit.

WALK 25

Tejeda and Cruz de Tejeda

Start/Finish	Tejeda
Distance	7km (4½ miles)
Total Ascent/Descent	500m (1640ft)
Time	2hrs 30mins
Terrain	Fairly easy winding paths and tracks, with some road-walking, on rugged slopes of bushy scrub.
Refreshments	Bars at Tejeda and Cruz de Tejeda.
Transport	Occasional daily buses link Tejeda and Cruz de Tejeda from San Mateo, San Bartolomé and Maspalomas.

The mountainside village of Tejeda is interesting and attractive, and is linked to Cruz de Tejeda by a convoluted road. Walkers can follow an old highway from the village up to Cruz de Tejeda. After exploring, another old highway can be followed back down to the village, making a largely traffic-free circuit.

Route uses PR GC 40.

Tejeda, at around 1050m (3445ft) (bar/restaurants, accommodation, shops, post office, bank with ATM; there is a tiny bus station as well as taxis), is roughly in the middle of Gran Canaria, clinging to the side of a deep barranco. The church of Nuestra Señora del Socorro is a prominent feature, and there are two museums and a centre for medicinal plants.

Start in the centre and use either the main road or one of the quiet roads running parallel to leave the village, but be sure to join and follow the road signposted 'Cruz Tejeda', running uphill. This eventually reaches a small **roundabout**. Just above it, a concrete track heads left. Almost immediately, turn right up a track parallel to the road. It ends suddenly and a winding path climbs onwards, sometimes with aloes alongside.

At a higher level the path appears to join the road near **Montaña de las Arenas**. There is no need to touch the road, but continue winding uphill, later passing an almond tree to join the road. Turn left up the road a few paces and cross over to find the path climbing higher. It is less well trodden, following a line of telegraph poles up a bushy slope and over a hill. Go down to a road junction and turn round the bend signposted 'Cruz Tejeda'. Pick up a good path that climbs and winds towards pines, reaching a road at

Cruz de Tejeda, around 1510m (4955ft). There are two hotels – the Parador and El Refugio – as well as souvenir stalls and Canarian food products on sale. ▶

Walks 3, 7, 8, 42 and 43 also start and/or finish here.

The Barranco de Tejeda and Roque Bentayga, seen on the climb to Cruz de Tejeda

Aloes stand to attention in front of the mighty Roque Bentayga above the Barranco de Tejeda

Climb straight uphill beside El Refugio, signposted as the PR GC 40 for Llanos de la Pez. A short way above the hotel grounds is a path junction, so turn right to start the descent to Tejeda. The path is often grassy on a slope of broom, narrowing beside a cliff, and passing a curious cave house. Drop to a road and cross it, walking a short way downhill to reach the road again. Turn left along the road and find a path heading down to the right. It is still grassy and is later flanked by dense tagasaste and tabaibal. Reach a road junction and bus shelter and turn left as signposted for Tejeda.

Turn right along a broad track serving **Finca La Isa**. This splits after a slight rise, so keep right downhill, flanked by stone walls, bushy scrub and almond trees. The surface is grassy, hiding uneven stones. There is a slight rise to pass a pylon, then go straight downhill, keeping just left of a farmhouse, to reach a road junction. Walk down a road serving a **helipad**, but head right down a concrete road before reaching it. This becomes a track, narrowing to a winding path further downhill. Rugged, boulder-strewn slopes feature tabaibal, verode, aloes, incienso and almond trees. Walk down to the main road in **Tejeda**, and return to the centre of the village to finish.

WALK 26
Tejeda and La Culata

Start/Finish	Tejeda
Distance	9km (5½ miles)
Total Ascent/Descent	500m (1640ft)
Time	3hrs
Terrain	Mostly clearly marked paths, tracks and roads on the slopes of a steep and rugged barranco.
Refreshments	Bars at Tejeda and La Culata.
Transport	Occasional daily buses serve Tejeda from San Mateo, San Bartolomé and Maspalomas. Buses sometimes detour to La Culata.

This route could be shortened by starting at a lower level in the Barranco de Tejeda (the bus can drop you off there), rather than in Tejeda, but the village is well worth exploring before or after the walk. Paths leading to and from La Culata are very scenic and the little village occupies a splendid site in a deep barranco.

Start in the centre of **Tejeda**, around 1050m (3445ft). Use either the main road or a quiet road running parallel to leave the village, down into the **Barranco de Tejeda**, around 1000m (3280ft). ▸ Most of the way down the road, there are views of Roque Nublo, Roque Bentayga and Altavista. A signpost for the PR GC 80 points back up the road, and left down a stone-paved track to a river.

Cross a concrete culvert bridge and follow the track upstream. Note a signposted path on the right, which is used later in the day. Watch for a ford and cross the river to reach a track on the other side. Follow it upstream, but quickly turn left up a rugged, boulder-paved path in a streambed. ▸

Wooden arrows on posts help enormously while following the path uphill, as there are junctions with

Route uses PR GC 80.

Starting here saves 3km (2 miles) in total.

Following the track to its very end reveals a waterfall in a rocky gully.

145

Huge boulders and little buildings deep in the Barranco de Tejeda

other paths and tracks on the steep, scrub-covered slope. Whenever there is a choice, the path to follow is the most well trodden. The first track crossed is marked as private, so continue straight uphill. The next track is concrete, and by turning left up it, the path is seen again and quickly leads up to a tarmac road. Turn right to follow the road, which bends and gently undulates across the steep valley sides, reaching **La Culata**, around 1220m (4000ft). Pass the church and note the PR GC 80 signposted down to the right, for Cruz de Timagada. ◄

Alternatively, continue towards two bars for refreshment, returning to the signpost afterwards.

The path drops steeply, with concrete giving way to boulder paving. Cross a concrete footbridge over a stream and climb a stone-paved path. Drift right and level out, then head up to a concrete road. Turn left and quickly right, as signposted, up to a house. Continue along a path into a bushy barranco where there might be a small waterfall. Rise gently across a slope of bushy scrub, including almonds, aloes and broom, with increasing numbers of tagasaste trees. There is a gentle descent past rock-fall boulders north of Roque Nublo. A three-way signpost for the PR GC 80 is reached.

A low-slung midday rainbow spans the barranco below La Culata

It is worth continuing straight ahead, making a short and gentle climb to a bare, gritty gap at **Cruz de Timagada**, at 1282m (4206ft). There is a small altar on the gap, fine views beyond and a monstrous tower of rock above. ▶

A short descent on a concrete path leads to a road with an occasional bus service.

Retrace steps to the three-way signpost and go down the winding, stone-paved path for Tejeda. The rugged slope supports almonds and aloes, with broom and tabaibal too. Cross a small barranco and climb a little, then continue downhill and go straight ahead past a couple

Tejeda

SF

Walk 26

Barranco de Tejeda

Helipad
Sports
Ground

Las Casa
del Lomo

N

Cruz de
Timagada

Walk 26

1282m

La Culata
La
Ortiguilla

147

of properties where there is a signpost. Stout fencing has been erected at the top of a stabilised slope. A final, winding, boulder-paved path leads back into the Barranco de Tejeda. Turn left to reach the road, then right to follow the road up to **Tejeda**.

WALK 27
Degollada Becerra and La Culata

Start/Finish	Degollada Becerra
Distance	9km (5½ miles)
Total Ascent/Descent	650m (2130ft)
Time	3hrs
Terrain	Clear paths, mostly marked and signposted, with some steep and rugged stretches on forested and rocky slopes.
Refreshments	Restaurant at Llanos de Garañón. Bars at La Culata.
Transport	Occasional daily buses serve Cruz de Tejeda, 2.5km (1½ miles) from Degollada Becerra, from Tejeda, San Bartolomé, Maspalomas and San Mateo. Buses sometimes detour into La Culata.

This short circular route is easy at first, but later descends steep and rugged to La Culata before climbing back to the start. It can be combined with Walk 28 to Roque Nublo, and/or around it, before descending to La Ortiguilla. It is possible to finish at La Culata by catching a bus, but study the limited timetable.

Route includes PR GC 40 and PR GC 60.

Start at **Degollada Becerra**, a roadside gap at 1548m (5079ft). Admire views of Roque El Fraile, Roque Nublo, Roque Bentayga, Altavista and distant El Teide on Tenerife. A path leads to a nearby visitor centre that might well be closed. Climb steeply from the gap on a crest of broom and pine. The path later runs gently along the crest, parallel to the road, passing right of a well-appointed house.

Another path rises from La Culata (used later in the day), and the route almost touches the nearby road.

Climb from a signpost, winding past broom and pines. Looking ahead, **Montaña del Andén del Toro** looks formidable, but it isn't climbed. Instead, the path drifts right and traverses its rugged slopes. Pass a cave and head downhill a little, forking right as marked. Climb gently through pine forest and cross a track as signposted on a crest. Go down the other side and cross another track in a level area. Further along, go through a gap in a low wall and turn left to follow the wall down to another track.

Turn right to follow the track, passing a sports ground before reaching a signposted junction at **Llanos de Garañón**, around 1670m (5480ft). Walk 30 continues straight ahead, and the PR GC 60 is signposted left and right. Left can be used to reach a large forest campsite and a restaurant. To continue the walk, however, turn right as signposted for La Goleta.

The path is broad and easy as it runs beside a wall and fence, but when it turns left downhill it becomes rugged and bouldery. When it levels out, it is worth wandering to the right for a fine view towards Roque Nublo. The path continues down through pine forest and crosses the dam of a small reservoir, **Presa de los Hornos**, flanked by gnarled rocky outcrops. Climb to reach a road, where there is access to a bare rock hump offering splendid views. Walk down the road to reach small car parks, signposts and a map-board at **La Goleta**. Various ramifications of the PR GC 60 are explained here: a simple there-and-back route to Roque Nublo, a circuit round the

The little reservoir of Presa de los Hornos lies surrounded by forest

Left is an arduous climb to Roque Nublo.

slopes supporting the rock, and paths down to Ayacata, El Aserrador and La Culata, see Walk 28.

To walk directly to La Culata, drop to the right as signposted. The path is rugged and winding, with stone paving and stone steps in places. The steep slopes are forested and littered with big boulders. Eventually, a three-way signpost for the PR GC 60 is reached. ◄ Turn right and walk quickly down to a concrete road and a map-board at **La Ortiguilla**. Walk down the steep concrete road, turning right onto a tarmac road, which rises and falls to **La Culata**. There are two bars close together, with a bus shelter and turning space beyond.

To continue, pass the first bar and turn right before the second, climbing a steep, winding, concrete path with steps and handrails, passing several houses. Cross a narrow road and continue straight up a short path to a concrete road. Turn left up this, then right along a cobbled path beside a house, levelling out on a terrace. Turn right up another cobbled path, which eventually joins a

tarmac road. Turn right up the road, and left up a concrete road, to reach a house called **La Palmita**.

Go straight up a clear path, zigzagging towards pines. Contour easily round a steep slope, crossing watercourses where willow grows. The path climbs a little and runs under a pipeline, then contours again. Keep right at a fork, up a winding, boulder-paved path. This turns a number of broad bends before reaching a gap and a road. Either turn left down the road to return quickly to **Degollada Becerra**, or turn left just before the road to retrace the earliest steps of the day back to the start.

A broad, rugged path climbs from La Culata to Degollada Becerra

151

WALK 28
Roque Nublo from La Goleta

Start/Finish	La Goleta, above Ayacata
Distance	5km (3 miles)
Total Ascent/Descent	350m (1150ft)
Time	2hrs
Terrain	Some paths are stone-paved or stony, while bare rock is crossed on higher parts. Some short stretches are steep, but most stretches are gentle.
Refreshments	Bar off-route at Ayacata.
Transport	Occasional daily buses serve Ayacata, 1.5km (1 mile) from La Goleta, from Maspalomas, San Bartolomé, Tejeda and San Mateo.

A simple there-and-back path allows walkers to get close to the mighty Roque Nublo, but only rock-climbers can reach the summit. It is worth completing a short circular walk round the rocky, forested slopes supporting the rock. Extensions are possible, linking with Walk 27 or Walk 29.

Route includes PR GC 60.

Start at a car park at **La Goleta**, above Ayacata, at 1578m (5177ft). A map-board shows various short paths that make up the PR GC 60, to and around Roque Nublo, with links to nearby villages. Roque Nublo is signposted along a broad, easy, buttressed path across a rugged slope of lumpy agglomerate. There is a view down to Ayacata, while ahead rise the striking pinnacle of El Fraile and the monstrous tower of Roque Nublo.

The circuit round Roque Nublo returns to this point.

The path enters pine forest and views are lost. At a higher level the path has been chiselled from the bedrock and rises to a junction. Left is for Roque Nublo, while right is signposted for La Culata. ◄ Further uphill, the path reaches a rocky gap where there is another signpost. Left is signposted for La Culata and right is for Roque Nublo. The path climbs on bare rock and has been cut deep to reach a broad, bare rock slope. Straight ahead is **Roque Nublo**,

rising to 1813 m (5948ft), flanked by a lesser tower. Study these closely by scrambling past boulders. ▶

Return to the signpost on the rocky gap to start a short circular walk. Turn right down a stony path as signposted for La Culata. This winds down a rugged, bushy, forested slope and eventually reaches a three-way signpost. Left is for El Aserrador, while right is for La Culata. Pass bushy scrub and sparse pines below Roque Nublo, rising gently among big boulders with views into the Barranco de Tejeda. Descend gently to another three-way signpost. Left offers a descent to La Culata (via the link route shown on the map) while walking ahead uphill is for La Goleta.

Only rock climbers can reach the top, which was first gained in 1932.

A breach has been hammered out of bedrock so that walkers can easily approach Roque Nublo

The path undulates across a bouldery, forested slope, and climbs back to the first signpost that indicated La Culata. Keep straight ahead and downhill, retracing earlier steps to return to the car park at **La Goleta**.

WALK 29
Cruz Grande to Ayacata

Start	Cruz Grande
Finish	Ayacata
Distance	9km (5½ miles)
Total Ascent	460m (1510ft)
Total Descent	410m (1345ft)
Time	3hrs
Terrain	A steep climb on a mountain path, then forested slopes. A road-walk and a winding path are used for the descent.
Refreshments	Bar at Ayacata.
Transport	Occasional daily buses serve Cruz Grande and Ayacata from Maspalomas, San Bartolomé, Tejeda and San Mateo.

A splendid stone-paved path climbs from Cruz Grande, picking out breaches in cliffs to reach high pine forests. A road-walk links with an old path at La Goleta for a descent to Ayacata. Walk 28 can be used to include a visit to Roque Nublo, if time allows before a bus needs to be caught.

Route uses PR GC 40 and PR GC 60.

Start at **Cruz Grande**, where a road bends through a rock cutting, around 1250m (4100ft). Signposts are located on both sides of the cutting, so find one on the San Bartolomé side, for the PR GC 40 to Llanos del Garañón. A stone-paved track leads up to a house, where a rugged stone-paved path climbs further. A rough and rocky ridge rises, with scrubby slopes, and the path goes on top of it a couple of times. Look back to see San Bartolomé, and look ahead to spot apparently impassable cliffs towering above.

A splendid, stone-paved path climbs from Cruz Grande, sometimes beneath overhanging cliffs

Map continues on page 157

Turn left to traverse beneath a cliff, passing almond trees and bushy scrub. The cliffs sometimes overhang, but a splendid, stone-paved path with impressive buttresses starts zigzagging and exploiting rocky breaches. A small reservoir is perched on a shelf to the left, and views expand as the zigzags climb higher and higher, passing a stand of pines and clumps of bushes on largely rocky slopes. The path straightens out and the stone paving ends near a shallow valley at **Pargana**, around 1600m (5250ft).

155

A path rises across bare rock and stony slopes towards pine forest at Pargana

Continue a gentle ascent across bare rock through the valley, where a strip of vegetation follows a small stream. Enter pine forest and cross more bare rock, later passing above a barranco with a view down to San Bartolomé and the distant coast. The path is well-constructed across rocky slopes, but less clear later, still beside the barranco. Climb among pines and broom on a path worn to earth or bedrock, later stone-paved, reaching a junction on a forested crest over 1700m (5580ft). ◄

Walk 30 can be followed right for Pico de las Nieves.

Walk straight ahead to descend through the forest onto bare rock, where there are views of a reservoir with Moriscos far beyond. Go down a stone-paved path and steps, crossing a streambed in a gentle dip in the forest. A low wall accompanies the broad path, often worn to bedrock, down to a road. ◄ Turn left and follow the bendy road, sometimes with a view of **Presa de los Hornos** below. There is a pronounced left bend where a hump of bare rock lies to the right, before the road reaches car parks at **La Goleta**, at 1578m (5177ft). A map-board shows various short paths that make up the PR GC 60, to and around Roque Nublo, with links to nearby villages. ◄

Walking straight ahead leads to Llanos de Garañón and a forest campsite.

If time can be spared, link directly with Walk 28 and visit Roque Nublo.

A signpost points along a clear path towards Roque Nublo, but almost immediately a rugged path drops steeply to the left. Follow it and later swing right to descend parallel to the road. Turn right down the road, watching for a signpost on the left for Ayacata. The path through pines and scrub becomes a boulder-strewn groove, later passing between buildings. Go down stone steps to a road and turn left to walk down to a house and signpost.

Go down a path with old, rugged paving, passing almond trees, broom and tagasaste. Drop between massive boulders and meander down an old, worn path. Go down a narrow access road and clip a road bend, where a signpost points down a path passing a tall pine. Turn quickly right and left when a concrete track is reached, and go down another rugged, worn path. This becomes a concrete track down to a road, and the road reaches **Ayacata** around 1300m (4265ft). There is a bar, bus stops and a small chapel.

Looking down towards the little mountain village of Ayacata

WALK 30

Llanos de Garañón and Pico de las Nieves

Start/Finish	Llanos de Garañón
Distance	11km (7 miles)
Total Ascent/Descent	350m (1150ft)
Time	3hrs 30mins
Terrain	Clear forest paths for the ascent, steep at times, followed by road-walking for the descent.
Refreshments	Bar/restaurants at Llanos de Garañón and La Cumbre.
Transport	None.

Motorists can drive onto Pico de las Nieves, the highest point on Gran Canaria – or as far as allowed by the military, who maintain a radar installation on the summit. A path can be followed from Llanos de Garañón, up steep, forested slopes to the summit, linking with high-level roads for an easy descent.

Route uses PR GC 40 and PR GC 10.

There are no buses to **Llanos de Garañón** but there is a campsite, where walkers might already be based, around 1670m (5480ft). Cars can be parked there, or at La Cumbre. There is a three-way signpost near the campsite access, and the PR GC 40 heads south for Cruz Grande. ◄ Walk down a broad, walled and fenced track, rising a short way, then go down to a road and signpost. Turn right to walk beside the road, first on the right, then on the left.

Walk 27 passes here, but follows the PR GC 60 to La Goleta.

A path on the left is signposted for Cruz Grande, as well as being the 'Camino de Santiago'. Follow the broad path, which is often worn to bedrock and has a low wall alongside, up a forested slope. Cross a streambed in a gentle dip, then follow a stone-paved path and steps, reaching bare rock. Look back to see Presa de los Hornos, with Moriscos far beyond. The path reaches a junction on a forested crest over 1700m (5580ft). ◄

Walk 29 also climbs to here, from Cruz Grande.

The summit radome on Pico de las Nieves is out of bounds to walkers, inside a military zone

Turn left and climb further up a forested slope, sometimes crossing bare rock, then as the slope steepens, the path drifts left to avoid cliffs. Climb steep and winding, reaching a bare rock crest with pines nearby on **Degollada de los Gatos**. The path continues uphill among pines, along a crest, then traverses left to avoid a rocky top at 1926m (6319ft). ▶ The traverse path drops to a forested gap, where a rocky promontory lies to the right.

Climb through the forest with some good views, reaching a road-end mirador that could be busy with motorists. There is no access to the summit of **Pico de las Nieves**, at 1949m (6394ft), which bears a large radome in a

Watch for lesser paths on the right, marked by cairns, to include this rocky top.

The view from the mirador on Pico de las Nieves, looking beyond Roque Nublo to El Teide on Tenerife

The road left can be used to short-cut downhill.

securely-fenced military zone. Walk down the road to a junction and turn right. ◄ A stone-paved path on the right leads quickly to a snow-pit called Pozo de Nieve Canónigos, but retrace steps afterwards. Watch for another stone-paved path on the left, heading down to a snow-pit called **Pozo de Nieve Grande**.

The continuation of the PR GC 10 to San Mateo.

Continue along this path (PR GC 10) as it continues down through forest, joining a track leading to a road. Turn left on the road soon passing the start of Walk 35. ◄ However, stay on the road, soon passing a junction where the short-cut joins. Follow the road onwards and there are sometimes opportunities to walk alongside, but only for short stretches on forested slopes. Eventually reach a crossroads at **La Cumbre**, around 1720m (5610ft). Turn left down the road for Ayacata, passing the Bar Restaurant La Cumbre. Turn right later to follow a dirt road back to **Llanos de Garañón**.

SAN BARTOLOMÉ

The steep and rocky Riscos de San Bartolomé rise to the highest mountains on Gran Canaria (Walk 31)

The delightful village of San Bartolomé is surrounded on most sides by steep and rugged mountains. The Riscos de San Bartolomé are a series of cliffs that bar direct access to Pico de las Nieves. However, the mountain can be climbed from Santa Lucía, and a descent can be made to Cruz Grande, linking with bus services, or keen walkers can continue all the way down to finish in San Bartolomé.

The municipality of San Bartolomé stretches all the way from the highest mountain on Gran Canaria, Pico de las Nieves, to the southern coast of the island. Within this area, a number of varied walks are offered. One is a circular walk from San Bartolomé, around steep, forested mountainsides, following good paths and forest tracks. Another route stretches from Ayagaures to Arteara, mostly following a clear and obvious convoluted dirt road. Far to the south, the shifting sand dunes at Maspalomas offer a short walk for anyone based in the tourist resorts.

Although walking routes seem sparsely spread in this section, it should be noted that Walks 44 and 45, later in this guidebook, offer a route from San Bartolomé to Maspalomas – from the high mountains to the gentle southern coast, linking all the walking routes in this area together.

WALK 31
Santa Lucía and Pico de las Nieves

Start	Santa Lucía
Finish	Cruz Grande
Distance	20km (12½ miles)
Total Ascent	1450m (4760ft)
Total Descent	880m (2890ft)
Time	8hrs
Terrain	Rugged paths on the ascent, often steep and winding, followed by easier tracks and a road to the top. Rugged paths on the descent, first through forest, then through breaches in cliffs.
Refreshments	Bars in Santa Lucía.
Transport	Occasional daily buses serve Santa Lucía and Cruz Grande from San Bartolomé.

This is a long and arduous route over Pico de las Nieves, outflanking the awesome, tiered cliffs of Riscos de San Bartolomé. There are buses serving either end, but start early and maintain a good pace to fit in with timetables. Alternative finish points can be considered with reference to nearby routes.

Route uses PR GC 30 and PR GC 40.

Start as early as possible in **Santa Lucía**, around 700m (2295ft) (bank with ATM, bar/restaurants, shops and buses). A park lies between two halves of the village, where steps climb to the church. Walk down the stone-paved Calle Senador Castillo Olivares, overlooking the park, watching on the left for a narrow gap between houses, signposted PR GC 30 for La Calderilla. Climb a stone-paved path and keep left, following a fence up a steep slope. Keep climbing to pass beneath a power line, levelling out among tabaibal and flowery scrub, following a narrow path flanked by low walls. Pass a signpost and look ahead to spot more signposts, keeping left of a fenced enclosure. Go down and up a path past old terraces, down and up again across a slope.

Looking towards the Riscos de San Bartolomé from the path above Taidia

Join a clear track and turn left to follow its undulating course across the slope. Note a solitary **orange house** below, and a fenced enclosure of almond trees to the left of the track. Just beyond the enclosure is a signpost, indicating a right turn along a narrow path. Head gently down beside houses at **Taidia**, over 850m (2790ft). Keep right at a path junction, gently rising, and turn right up a steep concrete road as signposted. Keep left at a junction, climbing and turning left to level out. The road descends gently to a house, then turn right up a few steps immediately afterwards.

The path is roughly stone-paved or rocky as it winds up a slope with fine views of tiered cliffs. The scrub includes tabaibal, verode, broom, calcosas, tajinaste and lavender, dotted with aloes and tagasaste. Climb past a shoulder bearing small fields, then the scrub is dense and bushy on the steep slope, with a few almond trees. Squeeze through the scrub while zigzagging

Map continues on page 165

A rocky peak protrudes from Pico de las Nieves, overlooking the Riscos de San Bartolomé

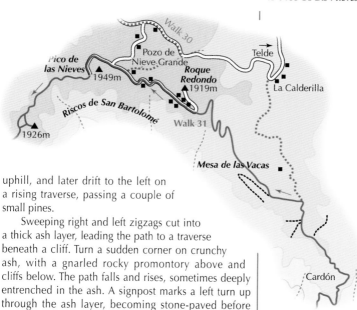

uphill, and later drift to the left on a rising traverse, passing a couple of small pines.

Sweeping right and left zigzags cut into a thick ash layer, leading the path to a traverse beneath a cliff. Turn a sudden corner on crunchy ash, with a gnarled rocky promontory above and cliffs below. The path falls and rises, sometimes deeply entrenched in the ash. A signpost marks a left turn up through the ash layer, becoming stone-paved before winding up a slope of dense scrub, giving way to broom at **Cardón**. The path joins a track at a signpost and turning space, entering pine forest around 1600m (5250ft).

Follow the gently undulating track to a junction, turn left and climb steeply, then gently. A couple of tracks head left in quick succession, so keep straight ahead, reaching a drystone sheepfold and a three-way signpost at a junction. Turn left for Pico de las Nieves. ▸ The track undulates through forest, then keep right at a junction on **Mesa de las Vacas**. Rise from the forest and traverse above the cliffs, with splendid views southwards.

The track later climbs more steeply, swings right, then left across the high crest on gentler slopes. Continue climbing and winding uphill, in and out of pine forest. When a road bend is reached below a series of red and white communication masts on **Roque Redondo**, keep left and pass below the masts. Cross a forested crest to pass smaller masts and concrete huts. Cross a gentle gap

Map continues on page 166

Straight ahead offers an exit to La Calderilla and a road.

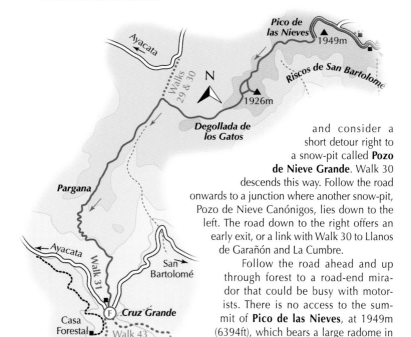

and consider a short detour right to a snow-pit called **Pozo de Nieve Grande**. Walk 30 descends this way. Follow the road onwards to a junction where another snow-pit, Pozo de Nieve Canónigos, lies down to the left. The road down to the right offers an early exit, or a link with Walk 30 to Llanos de Garañón and La Cumbre.

Follow the road ahead and up through forest to a road-end mirador that could be busy with motorists. There is no access to the summit of **Pico de las Nieves**, at 1949m (6394ft), which bears a large radome in a securely-fenced military zone. Views are good, but limited because of the forest. Walk down from the road, through the forest, to a gap where a rocky promontory lies to the left. Follow the path onwards, traversing across a slope to avoid a rocky top at 1926m (6319ft). ◄ Descend along a crest among pines, reaching a bare gap at **Degollada de los Gatos**. The path rises gently, then drops steep and winding, sometimes on bare rock, avoiding cliffs to the left. There are a couple of open areas before the path descends to a junction on a forested crest over 1700m (5580ft). ◄

Turn left down to **Cruz Grande**, following Walk 43, to catch a bus. If the last bus has gone, continue to follow Walk 43 all the way down to San Bartolomé.

Watch for lesser paths on the left, marked by cairns, to include this rocky top.

Turning right, Walk 29 leads to Ayacata and Walk 30 to Llanos de Garañón.

WALK 32

San Bartolomé and Cruz Grande

Start/Finish	San Bartolomé
Distance	14km (8¾ miles)
Total Ascent/Descent	400m (1310ft)
Time	4hrs
Terrain	Mostly good paths and tracks, occasionally steep and rugged, largely on forested slopes.
Refreshments	Plenty of choice in San Bartolomé.
Transport	Occasional daily buses serve San Bartolomé and Cruz Grande from Maspalomas, Tejeda and San Mateo.

Morro de la Cruz Grande is a rugged, forested mountain lying west of San Bartolomé. Good tracks and paths encircle it, offering a splendid circuit that is quite scenic, despite the forest, and often seems quite remote. Old mule paths are used at the start and finish, with gentle forest tracks in the middle.

Start at the church in the middle of **San Bartolomé**, around 900m (2950ft) (hotel, pensión, banks with ATMs, post office, shops, bars, restaurants, buses and taxis). Walk into the village and turn right up the brick-paved Calle Padre Claret. Turn left up the tarmac Calle del Corazón de Jesús. Turn right up Calle San Juan, which turns left and right with a view of the village and mountains. Turn left up Calle El Roque, which levels out to reach a junction. Turn right as signposted for Tejeda along Calle Manuel Zenón Araño Yánez. Turn left as signposted PR GC 40 for Cruz Grande, along Calle Juglar Fabian Torres.

This is a flat area with a **sports ground** nearby, and another signpost points right along the Camino Real Cruz Grande Cumbre. Follow a track flanked by pine trees, which soon rises and heads left, so keep straight ahead as signposted up a stone-paved path with steps. This climbs and winds on a rocky, pine-forested slope. Zigzag steeply

Route uses PR GC 40.

Walk 29 starts here.

uphill, then make gentler rising and falling traverses. A final series of winding climbs reveal fine views, then left and right turns up a track lead to a road and rock cutting at **Cruz Grande**, around 1250m (4100ft). ◄

Signposts are located on both sides of the cutting, so pass through to the Ayacata side, where the PR GC 40 is signposted left up a track for Degollada de la Manzanilla. The track rises and falls gently, hacked and bulldozed from a steep forested slope. Always stay on the track, avoiding the **Casa Forestal** down to the right, and an old path rising on the left. The track generally rises and there is a signpost on one bend, and another signpost at a later

The path descending from the gap at Degollada de la Manzanilla

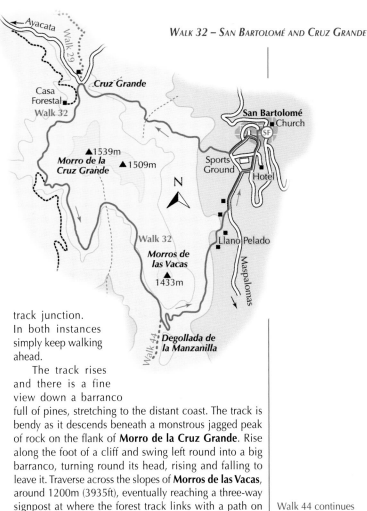

track junction.
In both instances
simply keep walking
ahead.

The track rises
and there is a fine
view down a barranco
full of pines, stretching to the distant coast. The track is
bendy as it descends beneath a monstrous jagged peak
of rock on the flank of **Morro de la Cruz Grande**. Rise
along the foot of a cliff and swing left round into a big
barranco, turning round its head, rising and falling to
leave it. Traverse across the slopes of **Morros de las Vacas**,
around 1200m (3935ft), eventually reaching a three-way
signpost at where the forest track links with a path on
Degollada de la Manzanilla. ▶

Walk 44 continues
straight ahead.

Turn left as signposted for the PR GC 40 to San
Bartolomé. Go down a winding, stone-paved or stone-
strewn path, noting massive stone buttresses holding
it in place. There are only a few pines, while the scrub
includes calcosas, tajinaste, tabaibal, broom, aloes and

lavender. The path is gentler as it runs along the base of a cliff, exploiting a soft, creamy layer of rock, sometimes beneath big overhangs. When the path turns left round a corner there are tottering pinnacles of rock above. The path is broad but suffers rock-falls and can't be used by vehicles. After crossing scree the track descends, with a farm to the right and forest left.

A junction is reached at **Llano Pelado**, so turn left as signposted, down a concrete track, continuing as a stony track down to a tarmac road. Turn left as signposted for San Bartolomé, which is also the 'Camino de Santiago'. Follow the road along and gently downhill. Keep straight ahead as signposted where a track joins from the left.

Tottering pinnacles of rock above the path on the way towards Llano Pelado

Next, turn right at a road junction, then left at the next junction, along the Avenida Teniente Alcalde Antonio Santana. There are turnings left for the sports ground and right for the Hotel Las Tirajanas, but keep straight ahead. Follow Calle El Roque and retrace the earliest steps of the day down into **San Bartolomé** to finish.

WALK 33

Arteara to Ayagaures

Start	Arteara
Finish	Ayagaures
Distance	15km (9½ miles)
Total Ascent	175m (575ft)
Total Descent	225m (740ft)
Time	5hrs
Terrain	Apart from rugged paths at the start, most of the route is along an easy dirt road with gentle gradients, crossing barren ridges and barrancos.
Refreshments	Bars at Arteara and Ayagaures.
Transport	Regular daily buses serve Arteara from Maspalomas and San Bartolomé. Taxi from Ayagaures to Maspalomas.

There is an interesting archaeological area at Arteara, where the original Guanche inhabitants of Gran Canaria cremated and buried their dead. Beyond lies a winding dirt road, crossing rugged ridges and deep barrancos. It is easy to follow, but a pick-up or taxi needs to be arranged at Ayagaures.

Buses serve **Arteara**, around 350m (1150ft), where the Camel Park has a restaurant. Follow a narrow road through the village, passing houses and prickly pears, looking at notices pointing out features of interest. A small car park lies at the end of the road, and a reception centre for the **archaeological park** lies up a few steps. To

The dirt road makes its way towards the Barranco de los Vicentillos

continue the walk, however, go up a short concrete path instead and head left along a rough and stony path.

Keep left at a path junction, marked as 'Tramo B Opcional'. Climb onto a raised viewing platform, scanning a mass of jumbled red rock

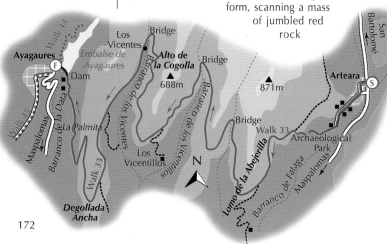

to spot as many cairns as possible, marking Guanche burials. The path runs into a stony dip, then winds uphill past scrub to reach a dirt road. Turn left up it, then follow it downhill. Two lesser tracks depart from it – one left and one right – but stay on the dirt road as it levels out. Note clumps of cardón on the slopes.

When a fork is reached around 400m (1310ft), keep right, rising and turning round the **Lomo de la Abejerilla**. The track has a stone-walled buttress alongside and later crosses a bridge over a streambed. Rise further and traverse round another crest, well above a gap around 450m (1475ft). The track descends and later levels out, crossing a bridge at a small dam in the **Barranco de los Vicentillos**. Rise again, and the track later splits, so keep right and rise gently. ▶

Left leads down to houses at Los Vicentillos.

Swing round the steep slopes into the Barranco de los Vicentes, descending gently and crossing it at a bridge flanked by masses of canes. There are a couple of houses and some fruit trees at **Los Vicentes**. The track runs gently down a short way, passing beneath a cliff, then climbs and passes cardón, reaching a gap at **Degollada Ancha**. A rocky peak is in view and as the track swings round to the

Looking down to a small reservoir and buildings at Los Vicentillos

right, look deep into the **Barranco de la Data**. The track climbs a little further then descends in a sweeping zig-zag around **La Palmita**. Finally pass between a couple of houses and cross the dam of the **Embalse de Ayagaures**. Turn left to walk into the village of **Ayagaures**, around 300m (985ft), where there is a bar.

There are no buses, but a taxi could be called for a run to Maspalomas. Alternatively, continue along Walk 45 for 12km (7½ miles) to Aqualand to catch a bus. There is no access from this route to buses at Palmitos Park.

WALK 34
Dunas de Maspalomas

Start/Finish	Faro de Maspalomas
Distance	6km (3¾ miles)
Total Ascent/Descent	30m (100ft)
Time	2hrs
Terrain	A short road-walk, followed by soft sand dunes, with the option of a sandy beach-walk.
Refreshments	Plenty of choice in Maspalomas and Playa del Inglés.
Transport	Regular daily buses serve Maspalomas from Las Palmas, the airport and most places in the south of Gran Canaria. Occasional daily buses serve Maspalomas from San Mateo, Tejeda and San Bartolomé.

The Dunas de Maspalomas is like a miniature desert between the busy resorts of Maspalomas and Playa del Inglés. It is flanked by a lagoon, golf course and the sea, and is protected as a nature reserve. Colour-coded trails cross it, and one stretch of the beach is used by naturists.

Start by facing the tall lighthouse of **Faro de Maspalomas** and the sea. Turn left to follow a tightly-squeezed coastal path on boards, cobbles and sand, past beach cafés and snack bars. Head inland along a broad, brick-paved

The landmark Faro de Maspalomas at the start of the low-level coast and dune walk

walkway beside the reed-beds and lagoon of **Charco**. Pass a viewing area equipped with notices explaining about the range of birds that can be seen on the nature reserve. The walkway continues inland and the reeds and woodlands become dense enough to hide the water. Turn right to

175

There is a view far inland to Pico de las Nieves – the highest mountain on Gran Canaria.

cross a bridge over a riverbed, passing a tall fence surrounding an area where camels are kept. ◄

Go through a gate, heading left, then right, to follow a hedge of prickly pears beside a golf course. Sandy paths are marked by yellow-banded posts, passing tamarisk bushes and tangled, spiky growths of aulaga. Looking ahead, buildings at **Playa del Inglés** are seen, and are reached by following blue/red-banded markers. A promenade path is reached near Riu Palace, where there is a botanic garden and an information centre for the nature reserve. Note how the dunes are now bare and devoid of vegetation cover.

There are two ways back to Maspalomas. One is to follow red-banded marker posts, but note that after heavy rain some parts might be covered in shallow pools of water. The vegetation cover increases along the way, and a footbridge spans a river-mouth at **Charco**. Simply retrace steps back to the prominent **Faro de Maspalomas**. Alternatively, head straight for the sea and turn right to follow the sandy beach (one stretch of the beach is used by naturists), before reaching the footbridge spanning the river-mouth.

Looking from the dunes near the coast, inland as far as the highest mountains on Gran Canaria

VALSEQUILLO

The village of Valsequillo is surrounded by signposted and waymarked walking routes (Walk 40)

The villages of Valsequillo, El Rincón and Tenteniguada are linked by interesting, signposted and waymarked PR (pequeño recorrido) routes, which continue climbing towards the high mountains. One of the features of walks from these villages is the enormous towers of rock that rise above the cultivated, terraced and forested slopes. These towers, or 'roques', appear to block access to the higher mountains, but there are steep and rugged paths passing around and behind them.

One of the routes in this section starts high in the mountains and descends to San Mateo, while another links San Mateo with Valsequillo, and yet another links Valsequillo with Santa Brígida. These village-to-village routes allow extended walks to be created, by joining them with some of the walks described at the beginning of this guidebook.

While some routes from the mountain villages can be combined to offer circular walks, paths can be very steep and tiring in places. Another route, from the Caldera de los Marteles to Valsequillo, runs mostly downhill. A drop-off would have to be arranged to complete this walk, since there are no bus services on the mountain road. However, the lower villages have very good bus links, with services operating early until late.

WALKING ON GRAN CANARIA

WALK 35
Siete Fuentes to San Mateo

Start	Siete Fuentes
Finish	San Mateo
Distance	8km (5 miles)
Total Ascent	1060m (3480ft)
Total Descent	55m (180ft)
Time	2hrs 30mins
Terrain	Easy tracks and steep paths on forested slopes lead to cultivated lower slopes with gentler tracks and roads.
Refreshments	Plenty of choice in San Mateo.
Transport	None to Siete Fuentes. Regular daily buses link San Mateo with Las Palmas.

The PR GC 10 starts at Pozo de Nieve Grande, high on Pico de las Nieves, with its initial descent covered by Walk 30. This continuation requires a drop-off on a high road, then a descent through forest, followed by well-settled slopes at a lower level. Roads eventually lead to San Mateo.

Route uses PR GC 10.

The start lies between Pico de las Nieves and La Calderilla, around 1830m (6005ft), near **Siete Fuentes**. A signpost for the PR GC 10 to San Mateo points along a track, down through pine forest and through a clearing. Pass a signpost and keep left a bit further down, also signposted. A short distance afterwards, turn right down a stone-paved path and steps, passing chestnut trees. Turn left as signposted down a track that leads to a ruin, but go down a path on the right beforehand, flashed yellow/white. There is a view down through a barranco, and the path winds past more chestnuts and broom.

Reach a track at a huddle of houses on a crest at **Hoya del Gamonal**. Walk down the track towards pines, turning left as signposted down a path, short-cutting a bend. Further down the track, turn left down another

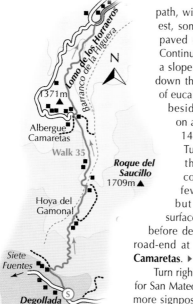

path, winding into forest, sometimes stone-paved or buttressed. Continue down across a slope of broom and down through a stand of eucalyptus, landing beside a signpost on a track, around 1400m (4595ft). Turn left down the track, on concrete past a few properties, but mostly unsurfaced. Rise gently before descending to a road-end at the **Albergue Camaretas**. ▶

Turn right as signposted for San Mateo, spotting two more signposts on the way

A huddle of buildings at Hoya del Gamonal, passed on the way down through a barranco

The view ahead stretches all the way to Las Palmas.

Map continues on page 180

179

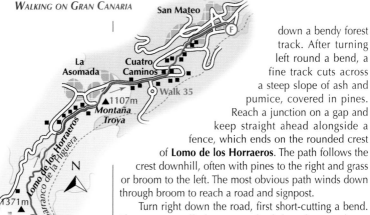

down a bendy forest track. After turning left round a bend, a fine track cuts across a steep slope of ash and pumice, covered in pines. Reach a junction on a gap and keep straight ahead alongside a fence, which ends on the rounded crest of **Lomo de los Horraeros**. The path follows the crest downhill, often with pines to the right and grass or broom to the left. The most obvious path winds down through broom to reach a road and signpost.

Turn right down the road, first short-cutting a bend. There are usually houses to the left and steep slopes planted with vines to the right, and later rampant scrub. When the road bends sharp left downhill, climb straight ahead, as signposted up a steep track on **Montaña Troya**. This soon levels out and a path leads downhill, flanked by tagasaste and broom. Go down a concrete road to a tarmac road and signpost. Follow the road ahead at **La Asomada**, over 1000m (3280ft), passing Viveres Odeja. Turn right down a concrete road as signposted. This becomes tarmac, reaching a main road. Walk straight ahead and pass a bus shelter, then turn left, unmarked, down a concrete road at **Cuatro Caminos**.

A path used on the lower slopes, around Montaña Troya, linking two roads

Cross the main road and go down a path. This becomes another concrete road called Cuesta Majorero. Cross the main road again and go straight down a quiet tarmac road, leading to the main road yet again. Either turn right and follow the main road into **San Mateo**, or cross the main road and go down Calle Cifuentes into the old part of town. Either way, turn right later to reach the bus station. For information about San Mateo, see the start of Walk 5.

WALK 36
San Mateo to Valsequillo

Start	San Mateo
Finish	Valsequillo
Distance	8km (5 miles)
Total Ascent	250m (820ft)
Total Descent	525m (1720ft)
Time	3hrs
Terrain	Roads, tracks and paths, sometimes on steep slopes, mostly through cultivated countryside.
Refreshments	Plenty of choice in San Mateo and Valsequillo.
Transport	Regular daily buses serve San Mateo and Valsequillo from Las Palmas. Occasional daily buses also link San Mateo and Valsequillo.

The walk from San Mateo to Valsequillo aims to link the remnants of the old mule paths that first linked the villages. Many have been superseded by tarmac roads, but some good examples remain. Part of this walk is shared with another village-to-village route – Walk 37 from Valsequillo to Santa Brígida.

Start at the bus station, which is on a gentle slope in **San Mateo**. See the start of Walk 5 for facilities. Leave the top end of it and keep left along roads, following Calle el Cantillo. This rises and falls, swinging left across a little

Route uses PR GC 11.

The Cruz, or cross, high above San Mateo, seen before heading along the Montañón road

barranco. Take a road up to the right, spotting a notice on a telegraph pole indicating Valsequillo. Apart from a dip near the beginning, the road climbs steeply and is flanked by tall walls, houses and cultivated plots. At the end of the tarmac, continue up a path often worn to bedrock, winding and climbing. The upper parts are stone-paved with tagasaste bushes alongside.

Reach a tarmac road around 1000m (3280ft) and turn left up the road. Just before the top, branch left along another road then left again. Walk down a track to a viewpoint and a prominent

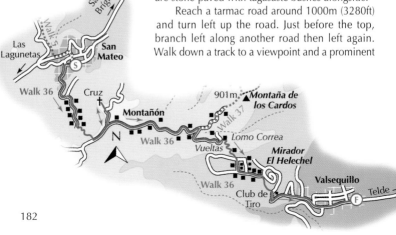

cross at **Cruz**. There is a bird's-eye view of San Mateo and the well-settled country rising from Las Palmas to the high mountains. The slopes are a tangled mass of aloes, prickly pears and incienso. Walk back along the track, right along the road, then left to follow the other road. This rises and falls, meandering from side to side along a crest at **Montañón**, past little houses. An unsightly pylon line marches the same way.

Eventually, there is a sudden right bend and a signpost, so turn right for the PR GC 11 to Valsequillo. ▸ Go down the bendy road, but watch carefully on a prominent left bend for a yellow/white flashed track down to the right. The track is partly stone-paved, more like a broad path, and it descends as sweeping zigzags at **Vueltas**. The steep slope is covered in aloes, prickly pears, tabaibal, verode and broom. There are fine views across the well-settled valley, which is full of cultivated terraces and plots, with high mountains beyond.

When a broader track is reached at the bottom, turn left down it, but not to the road. Instead, when the track becomes concrete, follow an old stone-paved path away from it, down between prickly pears to a road. Walk straight down the road, reaching a signpost at the bottom. Turn left and the road rises towards the prominent hill of **El Helechal**. ▸

Turn right along a stone-paved path before reaching a road junction, short-cutting down a rugged, scrubby slope to a lower part of the road. Turn right and left down the road, passing near a firing range, the **Club de Tiro**. Turn right down a road short-cutting steep and direct to **Valsequillo**. It reaches a plaza and viewpoint where there is a map-board detailing local walking routes. Follow the brick-paved Calle Leon y Castillo down to the church of San Miguel. Another map-board stands on Calle Isla de La Gomera, just to the left. Keep walking straight through town (accommodation, banks with ATMs, post office, shops, bar/restaurants, tourist information office, buses and taxis) to find bus stops around 550m (1805ft). ▸

Straight ahead is Walk 37 to Santa Brígida.

This can be climbed using a spiral road, to a summit viewpoint, and possibly, if work is completed, a bar/restaurant.

'Valsequillo' is a notable brand of cheese sold throughout the Canary Islands.

Valsequillo, as seen from the slopes of El Helechal, which can be climbed using a spiral road

WALK 37
Valsequillo to Santa Brígida

Start	Valsequillo
Finish	Santa Brígida
Distance	9km (5½ miles)
Total Ascent	450m (1475ft)
Total Descent	500m (1640ft)
Time	3hrs
Terrain	Roads, tracks and paths, sometimes on steep slopes, mostly through cultivated countryside.
Refreshments	Plenty of choice in Valsequillo and Santa Brígida. Bar at Cruz de Gamonal.
Transport	Regular daily buses serve Valsequillo and Santa Brígida from Las Palmas. There are also occasional buses from Valsequillo with San Mateo, linking with regular buses to Santa Brígida.

This village-to-village walk links a series of old mule paths, though some have been superseded by tarmac roads and tracks. After crossing an upland crest, the route drops and runs through a barranco, reaching a bar/restaurant on another crest before continuing down to Santa Brígida.

Start in **Valsequillo**, around 550m (1805ft), heading for the church of San Miguel. The brick-paved Calle Leon y Castillo climbs straight to a plaza and viewpoint. Keep climbing Calle Sol, maybe spotting a signpost for the PR GC 11. Continue up Calle La Orilla and head left up a steeper road. Turn left along a broader road, which makes a sharp right turn near a firing range, the **Club de Tiro**. Further up the road, watch for an old stone-paved path marked on the left, short-cutting up a slope of aloes, prickly pears, calcosas and tabaibal, scented with lavender and incienso. The path climbs to a road junction near the prominent hill of **El Helechal**. ▶

Route uses PR GC 11 and SL GC 07.

This can be climbed using a spiral road, to a summit viewpoint, and possibly, if work is completed, a bar/restaurant.

Turn left downhill, then right uphill from a sign-posted junction. When the road turns left, go straight up a path that becomes stone-paved, later flanked by prickly pears. Cross over a bendy concrete track and continue straight up another track, watching for markers on the right at **Vueltas**. A stone-paved path zigzags up a steep and scrubby slope, joining a road around 900m (2950ft). Keep left, in effect straight ahead, to climb the road to a junction. A signpost points right down a lesser road, indicating the SL GC 07.

Walk down the battered tarmac road into a dip, and continue along a winding track, rising and falling, roughly aligned to a broad crest. Avoid turnings and watch for green/white flashes across the slopes of **Montaña de los Cardos**. A waterhole (or mud-hole) appears on the right, and at this point, watch for a path on the left, marked with a green/white 'X'. The path often runs down bare rock, short-cutting a huge bend on the track. However, there are multiple paths further down, so take care. Don't return to the track, but keep left, picking up the only path down a slope of broom and other scrub.

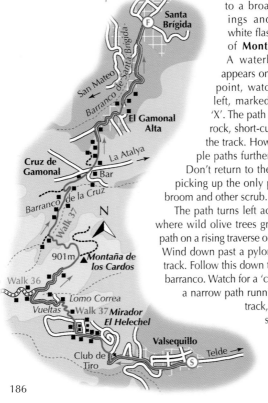

The path turns left across a little barranco where wild olive trees grow. Follow a narrow path on a rising traverse on a steep, bushy slope. Wind down past a pylon and join a concrete track. Follow this down through the bed of the barranco. Watch for a 'camino' sign indicating a narrow path running parallel to a stony track, beside a cane-choked streambed. Follow the track onwards, either concrete or stony, down to the

Walkers climbing a rugged path at Vueltas, high above Valsequillo

Looking down through the barranco to the distant Santa Brígida

Exotic garden plants can be admired on the way into Santa Brígida

Barranco de la Cruz, then up to **Cruz de Gamonal**. The Bar Restaurante Bernardino stands around 700m (2295ft).

Just across the road from the bar, a track runs downhill, becoming concrete as it bends left. Keep straight ahead along and down a clear path, becoming a track, joining a tarmac road. Continue down the road, flanked by fennel, reaching a junction overlooking the Barranco de Santa Brígida and an arched aqueduct. Turn right and follow a road, Camino del Gamonal, steeply downhill. It winds, rises and falls, then look out for a green-banded marker post on the left, beside a house numbered 28 at **El Gamonal Alta**.

Go down a path that varies from concrete and cobbles to trodden earth and rock, landing on a steep concrete road. Turn left down this, then right along a tarmac road overlooking oranges, lemons and palms. The meandering road becomes the Camino Palma Romero, reaching a main road at a large BP garage at **Santa Brígida** (shops, bars, post office, banks with ATMs, buses and taxis). Turn right to reach a busy junction where there are bus stops, over 500m (1640ft). Walk 1 finishes here and Walk 4 starts here.

WALK 38
El Rincón and Cuevas Blancas

Start/Finish	El Rincón
Distance	8km (5 miles)
Total Ascent/Descent	1250m (4100ft)
Time	4hrs
Terrain	Roads and tracks at the start and mid-way, but mostly steep and winding paths on well-vegetated or forested slopes.
Refreshments	Bar in El Rincón.
Transport	Occasional daily buses serve El Rincón from Telde and Valsequillo. A few buses serve El Rincón from San Mateo.

Steep and narrow paths climb above El Rincón, pushing through blue tajinaste bushes, with monstrous towers of rock above. The route almost reaches the waterless reservoir of Presa de Cuevas Blancas. Roque del Saucillo is passed as other tracks and paths are linked on the descent.

The highest bus shelter in **El Rincón** has map-boards beside it, around 920m (3020ft). Walk past the Bar Rincóncito to the end of Calle El Pino. Turn right at a junction, quickly climbing to another junction with signposts left and right – both indicating Cuevas Blancas. Turn left, along and down Calle Los Parrales, then rise to a junction and turn left to the end of the road. Turn right up the steep Calle El Roque Grande, with the rock itself high above. Wind steeply up to a sort of crossroads, map-board and three-way signpost beside a stout chestnut tree.

Walk straight ahead up a track, signposted as the SL GC 03 to Cuevas Blancas, passing the last couple of buildings, reaching a small turning space. A path rises steeply, sometimes wooded or scrubby, but mostly past blue tajinaste bushes. Old cultivation terraces are completely wild, with rocky ground rising high above. The

Route uses SL GC 01, SL GC 03 and SL GC 04.

Roque Grande is prominent on the climb from El Rincón to Presa de Cuevas Blancas

path winds, climbs and squeezes past rampant vegetation, drifting closer to the base of **Roque Grande**. Views stretch down through El Rincón and Tenteniguada to Valsequillo and distant Las Palmas.

A level, stone-paved area is reached beside a pine, and the path runs level past a cave on its way into a valley. Climb and wind steeply uphill again, often rugged underfoot, squeezing through bushy scrub. Trees give way to broom and blue tajinaste, and an old winch cable lies along the path on the way to a little gap behind **Roque del Pino**, over 1500m (4920ft). Turn left to climb along a crest of broom, where the path is narrow and winding, often worn

to bedrock, with log steps on steeper parts. The gradient eases as the path passes beneath a pylon line, rising to a forest and road. ▶

Map-boards and a signpost stand by the road, near the waterless **Presa de Cuevas Blancas**. Turn right and follow a path signposted as the SL GC 04, climbing a slope of broom beside a pine forest. Pass a trig point among the pines, at 1739m (5705ft), then drop into dense broom. Emerge to pass in front of a cave house, and turn left up a concrete track that later becomes stony, rising to a junction with another track. Turn right, down alongside pine forest, later entering it. Stay on the clearest track as marked, with patches of old stone paving, emerging from the forest overlooking Valsequillo and Las Palmas, with **Roque del Saucillo** towering above. Follow the track as it winds downhill, with a stand of pines to the left.

Watch for a green/white flashed path on the left, down along a crest of broom. Briefly re-join the track further down, then another path drops to the right, past

Turning left down the winding road leads, in 2km (1¼ miles), to Caldera de los Marteles, where Walk 39 or Walk 40 offer alternative descents.

Despite being flanked by dense vegetation, the path is obvious as it climbs

a few chestnuts, into broom and other scrub. The path winds down a steep and sometimes rocky, scrubby slope, then makes a downward traverse among pines. Continue down a rocky crest of pines and blue tajinaste, getting close to rock pinnacles. The path turns left to avoid the pinnacles, continuing down among pines, steep and narrow, cut into a damp slope.

Turn right at the bottom to pass a wall enclosing a deep hole. Follow the path down a slope of mixed scrub to a little gap and turn right as marked. The path is steep and crumbling, and blue tajinaste gives way to mixed scrub. The path is marked as it wanders down

Pinnacles of rock appear to block the descent to El Rincón, but the path skirts round them

between cultivated plots and terraces, reaching a concrete road and signpost. Turn left down the road, Calle Los Barrancos, to a junction with a tarmac road. Turn left down Calle El Toril, and left again at a signposted junction passed earlier in the day. Turn left along Calle El Pino, passing the Bar el Rincóncito, to finish back at the bus shelter in **El Rincón.** ▸

An alternative finish to Valsequillo is possible – see the end of Walk 39.

WALK 39

Tenteniguada and Caldera de los Marteles

Start/Finish	Tenteniguada
Alternative Finish	Valsequillo
Distance	12km (7½ miles); to Valsequillo: 15½km (10¼ miles)
Total Ascent/Descent	800m (2625ft); extra ascent/descent to Valsequillo: 50m (165ft)/300m (985ft)
Time	5hrs; to Valsequillo: 6hrs 15mins
Terrain	Steep, winding paths on rocky, well-vegetated slopes for the ascent and descent, with easier tracks on the highest parts.
Refreshments	Bars in Tenteniguada and El Rincón.
Transport	Occasional daily buses serve Tenteniguada and El Rincón from Telde and Valsequillo. A few buses serve Tenteniguada from San Mateo.

A steep and winding climb from Tenteniguada gives way to gentler slopes leading to a cultivated crater called the Caldera de los Marteles. The descent leads through forest and passes mighty towers of rock. After the return to Tenteniguada, an alternative finish is possible down to Valsequillo.

Tenteniguada stands at round 800m (2625ft), and the walk starts by heading down the main road towards Valsequillo (banks with ATMs, shops, bars and buses). The pavement is like a linear park with fine views, then the road bends round a barranco, reaching a bus shelter at a road

Route uses PR GC 12 and SL GC 01.

A family of prominent 'roques' tower high above Tenteniguada and El Rincón

Map continues on page 197

junction. Turn sharp right up Calle M Daniel Perez, signposted as the PR GC 12 for Caldera de los Marteles. There are a few houses to the left, a few almond trees to the right, and a level area at a cemetery. Keep climbing up the road, turning right at a junction, reaching a signpost where a track heads left.

Keep left, in effect straight uphill, to follow a path flashed yellow/white. The path often winds in a groove, and no matter how mixed or bushy the scrub becomes, there are always almond trees. The views on the ascent of **Los Alfaques** are dominated by Roque Grande to the right, while looking back, Las Palmas and La Isleta are seen as height is gained. The scrub later diminishes and the path reaches a gentle grassy crest, with pines down to the left, over 1200m (3940ft) at **El Espigón**.

The crest becomes a rocky, scrubby roller-coaster, but the path is always clear and avoids the humps. Old terraces can be seen all around, and the path drifts down from the crest and climbs to a track at a couple of buildings on a gap. Turn right up the bendy track, watching on the left for an indistinct short-cut up a grassy slope. Another short-cut heads to the left of a rocky little peak on a steep, rocky, bushy slope. Turn right again up the track at a gentle gradient, reaching a building and three-way signpost at **Orillones del Salviar**. ▸

Walk 40 descends to the left as the SL GC 02 to Valsequillo.

Follow the track ahead to a pine forest, up to a road on a gap, signposts and map-boards, around 1550m (5085ft) at **Caldera de los Marteles**. Enjoy views on both sides of the road, into the well-cultivated crater on one side, and as far as Las Palmas and La Isleta on the other.

The Caldera de los Marteles contains fertile plots, over 1500m (4920ft) above sea level

The winding road could be followed uphill for 2km (1¼ miles) to Presa de Cuevas Blancas, where Walk 38 offers an alternative descent.

Leave the road by following a bendy track down among pines, signposted as the SL GC 01 for El Rincón. The track continues uphill and levels out. Leave it and turn right down a path as marked, curving round the mountainside, mostly among broom, facing the back of Roque Grande. One stretch of the path across a sloping rock needs care, then climb a little onto a crest, and continue down through blue tajinaste bushes. The path descends towards pines, then drops into dense blue tajinaste and winds down a worn groove. Later, swing down into a steep valley, levelling out with **Roque Grande** towering above.

The path becomes bouldery and climbs a little, crossing crumbling ash and making a level traverse. Wind down among blue tajinaste and broom, passing tagasaste and almonds. Later, drop directly onto a concrete road at **La Umbría** and turn left to follow it downhill. Join a tarmac road at a three-way signpost and map-board beside

A track winds towards Roque Grande and a path traverses the rugged slopes

a stout chestnut tree. Turn right down a steep and wind-ing road, Calle El Roque Grande. Turn left along Calle los Parrales, which runs down, then up to a junction with signposts. Turn right downhill, then left along Calle El Pino, passing the Bar El Rincóncito in **El Rincón**.

The walk could be finished at a bus shelter and map-boards, around 920m (3020ft), otherwise continue down to a road junction and another bus shelter, noting massive walls supporting orange groves. Turn left as sign-posted for Tenteniguada and walk down a bendy road. A signpost on the right indicates a concrete path with railings to a road-end turning space. Continue down the road, Calle Las Portadas, into **Tenteniguada**. Don't turn left until forced to, then turn right at a junction, down Calle La Pelota, onto the main road.

Alternative finish at Valsequillo
Calle San Juan is signposted as the SL GC 05 to Valsequillo, and the little church of San Juan lies to the right, followed by the Casa de la Cultura and houses. Walk straight down the road, out of the village, with a cliff to the right. The road is often flanked by eucalyptus, reaching more houses. Continue along a narrow road, **Llanos de San Juan**, reaching a turning space where the road and houses finish.

Follow a rugged, boulder-paved path past aloes and eucalyptus. Turn right as marked down a narrower stone-paved path, which broadens as it winds down into a bar-ranco. The scrub is mixed, but notable for the amount of lavender. Cross the bed of the barranco, below 600m (1970ft), passing tall eucalyptus. Go up the other side, joining and fol-lowing a road,

A boulder perched above a barranco on the route from Tenteniguada to Valsequillo

For facilities see the end of Walk 36.

keeping left past houses at **Colmenar Alto**. Walk down to a road, where a bus shelter and bridge lie left, but cross the road and go down a signposted stone-paved path with steps.

Cross the bed of the **Barranco de San Miguel**, turning right as marked along a rugged stretch, then left up a steep and stony climb. Continue up a concrete track and a steep, brick-paved road to reach a main road and signpost. Cross over and walk up the brick-paved Calle Antonio Macia to the church of San Miguel in **Valsequillo**. Walk down from there to find bus stops, around 550m (1805ft). ◄

WALK 40

Caldera de los Marteles to Valsequillo

Start	Caldera de los Marteles
Finish	Valsequillo
Distance	12km (7½ miles)
Total Ascent	150m (490ft)
Total Descent	1150m (3775ft)
Time	4hrs
Terrain	Rugged paths in a deep, wooded barranco link with easy tracks and roads. Another barranco is crossed at the end.
Refreshments	Plenty of choice in Las Vegas and Valsequillo.
Transport	Regular daily buses serve Valsequillo from Las Palmas and Telde. Occasional daily buses link Las Vegas and Valsequillo.

This walk starts at Caldera de los Marteles (or serves as an alternative descent on Walk 38 or Walk 39) and the route explores the Barranco de los Cernícalos, then makes a rugged traverse along the base of a cliff. A good track leads to Las Vegas, then a barranco is crossed to Valsequillo.

Caldera de los Marteles lies between Telde and Pico de las Nieves, around 1550m (5085ft). Look into the well-cultivated crater on one side of the road, and as far as Las Palmas and La Isleta on the other. There are map-boards and signposts, so find the ones indicating the PR GC 12 and SL GC 02. Follow a track down through pine forest, emerging to reach a building and a three-way signpost at **Orillones del Salviar**. Turn right for the SL GC 02, signposted for Las Vegas and Valsequillo.

Walk downhill and take the second path to the right, flashed green/white. This runs down a groove worn to bedrock and boulders, then an easier path runs through broom and across grassy slopes, followed by tagasaste trees. Buildings come into view at **Cueva Blanca**, so

Route uses PR GC 12, SL GC 02 and SL GC 06.

A remarkably flowery traverse passes beneath the cliffs of Risco del Drago

when a track is reached, turn right towards them. Cross a narrow tarmac road and continue straight down another track, flashed green/white. ▶ Go down past a house and note some cave houses to the left. Wind down through tagasaste woods, with almond trees apparent later.

When the track makes a sudden left turn, a narrow path is flashed green/white down to the right. Follow it, squeezing through woods and scrub, down past a prominent eucalyptus to ford a jungle-like streambed. There are more almonds, and as the path runs onwards, the slopes are rockier and drier, with mixed flowery scrub. Pass a couple of caves beneath a small white building. Wind steeply down and cross the streambed again. Climb a little and continue down through dense woodland, crossing the streambed yet again. Walk up a little, then down the path and cross the streambed a fourth time. Cross the streambed a final time further down.

The path emerges on a drier slope of almonds, prickly pears, aloes and some particularly fine tabaibal. Despite a descent towards the **Barranco de los Cernícalos**, the path begins a rising traverse across a steep, rocky, scrubby slope. The amazingly mixed scrub includes prickly pears, aloes, tabaibal, calcosas, canes, wild olives and white tajinaste, scented with lavender and incienso. A pipeline lies buried under the path, which runs beneath the cliffs of **Risco del Drago**,

The 'prohibido el paso' notice applies only to vehicles.

Map continues on page 202

201

turning a corner around 1000m (3280ft) and catching a glimpse of Telde. The path continues easily, ending with a rocky climb to reach a bend on a track.

Turn right down the track, which is cut into an ash slope, descending in sweeping zigzags past broom and calcosas. It is stony and rocky further down, then climbs through a rock cutting on **Degollada Blanca**. Walk down the winding track, through another little rock cutting, down a slope of almonds and olives to a junction at **Los Mocanes**. Turn right along a tarmac road, Calle Las Haciendas, down to a junction and three-way signpost. Keep left down a road and cross a barranco, rising and falling to reach **Las Vegas**. Walk straight ahead at junctions to reach the main road, turning right to find map-boards and signposts.

Walk down the road, with bars and bus stops on both sides, to a left bend. A signpost for the SL GC 06 points right, down Calle F Diaz Beltrana. Pass a bar and turn left down Calle Nicolas Santana, reaching a three-way signpost. Turn left along a narrow path, with a wall to the left and a row of almond trees to the right. Cross a track and go straight down a narrow, winding path into the **Barranco de San Miguel**, below 500m (1640ft). Turn right down the bouldery bed, watching for markers where the path switches side to side. Once round a corner, watch for a marked and signposted path climbing left. This is rough and rocky, passing tabaibal and aloes, reaching a main road around 550m (180ft) in **Valsequillo** (accommodation, banks with ATMs, post office, shops, bar/restaurants, tourist information office, buses and taxis). ◄

A map-board and bus shelter are nearby.

202

GR 131 –
PUERTO DE LAS NIEVES TO MASPALOMAS

Walkers on the GR 131 follow a stone-paved path past a little reservoir high above Cruz Grande (Walk 43)

The GR 131 is an island-hopping trail stretching across all seven of the Canary Islands. Although the route has been fully signposted and waymarked on the neighbouring islands of Tenerife and Fuerteventura, work on Gran Canaria has yet to start. However, the rough outline of the route is known and, apart from the northern stretch, the following five-day route should be reasonably close to the coast-to-coast route from Puerto de las Nieves to Maspalomas.

From Puerto de las Nieves, the GR 131 may take a different route towards Artenara but, in the meantime, a splendid ridge walk can be followed to the forested uplands of Tamadaba, where there is a basic campsite. After passing Artenara,

the route takes a series of high-level paths to Cruz de Tejeda, where a couple of hotels sit on a mountain gap. Throughout the trail, links are possible with many other walking routes described in this guidebook.

The GR 131 will stay high on the mountain crest through Gran Canaria, passing fairly close to Pico de las Nieves before dropping to Cruz Grande and San Bartolomé. The mountains and barrancos beyond become increasingly arid on the way to the little village of Ayagaures. Beyond, the route is confined to roads but at least starts by following a fine mountain road. Towards the end, roadside paths are followed through the built-up resort of Maspalomas, ending at the tall landmark lighthouse of Faro de Maspalomas.

WALK 41

GR 131 – Puerto de las Nieves to Tamadaba

Start	Puerto de las Nieves
Finish	Campsite, Tamadaba
Distance	12km (7½ miles)
Total Ascent	1250m (4100ft)
Total Descent	50m (165ft)
Time	4hrs
Terrain	Stony paths and tracks as arid slopes become steeper. A steep and rocky climb leads to gentler paths and tracks through forested uplands.
Refreshments	Bar/restaurants at Puerto de las Nieves.
Transport	Regular daily buses serve Puerto de las Nieves from Las Palmas. Occasional daily buses serve Puerto de las Nieves from La Aldea. There are also daily ferry services from Tenerife.

This route is the most direct way from the coast at Puerto de las Nieves to the high mountains. It climbs arid, stony slopes, followed by a narrow path across a steep slope, linking with an old mule path climbing steep and rocky. A gentler continuation through pine forest leads to a campsite at Tamadaba.

Start from the ferryport at **Puerto de las Nieves**, following a promenade with views of El Teide and Tenerife. Walk straight inland from a roundabout, past the Hotel Puerto de las Nieves and a bus stop at the next roundabout. Continue to another roundabout featuring a huge metal map of Gran Canaria. The **Restaurante La Palmita** is across the road, with lovely gardens to explore. The main road bends left, and the road to La Aldea climbs right. Climb a stone-paved road above La Palmita and turn left up a stone-paved path with steps. This climbs a slope dotted with tabaibal, prickly pears and cardón. As height is gained, more of the coast and higher mountains are seen. Cross a road and continue up a stony track, passing a dump full of broken bottles.

The track winds up a scrubby slope and is very clear, splitting later. Small cairns mark a direct climb up a fine gravel track, rather than the stony track. Cross the stony track and continue uphill, later turning left to follow it. There is a gentle descent to a gap, reaching a ruined limekiln and an era. No doubt both took advantage of the breeze. A narrow, but clear path continues up past cardón, then tabaibal at a higher level. A rounded, gritty crest over 400m (1310ft) bears prickly pears and aulaga. The crest becomes steep and rocky at **La Higuera**.

A circular era and the ruins of a limekiln, both taking advantage of a crest with a breeze

Map continues on page 207

205

Steep and rugged slopes drop to the sea on the way to La Higuera

Watch for a very narrow path heading left, on a rising traverse between rocky ledges on a steep, grassy slope. This may be unsuitable for anyone suffering from vertigo, and no-one can afford to slip! Turn a corner and step up onto another rising traverse. One part drifts down a little, then up again, followed by a more direct climb up a wider path. Another rising traverse offers exceptional views, then later feathery tussocks of grass appear where old terraces are stacked on the mountainside, over 600m (1970ft). The path is safer, but still on a steep slope, meandering towards a gap. There is a path junction near **Roque Bermejo**, and a three-way signpost. ▶

Walk 13 joins from San Pedro.

Turn right as signposted for Tamadaba, climbing a narrow but clear path, passing tabaibal, cistus and bracken on slopes studded with big boulders. The cliffs above have no apparent breach, so the path is deflected to the right on a rising traverse until one appears. The path climbs through the breach and is stone-paved as it follows a rocky ridge, with cistus and rock-rose alongside. The final zigzags have stout buttresses, climbing to pine and eucalyptus as the path enters a forest, passing notices on **Montaña de las Presas**, over 1000m (3280ft).

Follow a gently undulating, but generally rising path through the forest, often cushioned with pine needles. Rise to a track and continue onwards and upwards. Always keep ahead and climb at junctions, no matter what other paths and tracks do. When the track does drop, at a number 7 marker, keep left to climb a clear, winding path. This becomes steep and stone-paved, with heather trees among pines, reaching a stony track. Turn right up the track, signposted for Artenara, and reach another signpost near a large **picnic site**, over 1200m (3940ft). Turn right to reach a basic forest **campsite**.

207

WALK 42

GR 131 – Tamadaba to Cruz de Tejeda

Start	Campsite, Tamadaba
Finish	Cruz de Tejeda
Distance	17km (10½ miles)
Total Ascent	1000m (3280ft)
Total Descent	670m (2200ft)
Time	6hrs
Terrain	Mostly high-level forest paths, tracks and roads, often gently graded, with only a few steep and rugged stretches, and some open slopes.
Refreshments	Bars at Artenara and Cruz de Tejeda.
Transport	Occasional daily buses serve Artenara from Las Palmas and Teror. Occasional daily buses serve Cruz de Tejeda from San Mateo, Tejeda, San Bartolomé and Maspalomas.

This stage runs more or less along the high, forested, mountainous crest of Gran Canaria. Paths miss the summits and often run parallel to roads, or even along them for short stretches. The attractive village of Artenara lies halfway to Cruz de Tejeda. There are links with many other walks in this book.

Backtrack from the **campsite** at Tamadaba to the large picnic site, over 1200m (3840ft). A path is signposted uphill for Artenara, rising and falling, but generally rising through dense pine forest hung with straggly skeins of lichen. Reach a three-way signpost and turn right up to a road at **Siete Pinos**. ◄ Turn left along the road, as signposted for Artenara and Cruz de Tejeda, bearing in mind that many more signposts point in that direction throughout the day. Don't go up a track on the right, but stay on the bendy road, and also avoid a path on the right. Instead, go down a path on the left, which soon rises back to the road.

Turn quickly left, then up to the right as signposted for Artenara, following a path that rises and falls beside

Walk 13 turns left downhill.

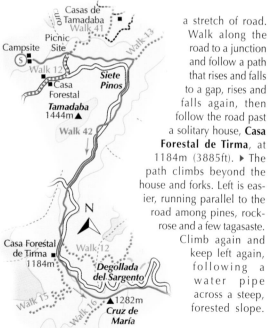

a stretch of road. Walk along the road to a junction and follow a path that rises and falls to a gap, rises and falls again, then follow the road past a solitary house, **Casa Forestal de Tirma**, at 1184m (3885ft). ▶ The path climbs beyond the house and forks. Left is easier, running parallel to the road among pines, rockrose and a few tagasaste. Climb again and keep left again, following a water pipe across a steep, forested slope.

A map-board at Degollada del Sargento, which is also the start of Walk 16

Walk 12, from Artenara to Tamadaba, and Walk 15, to Andén Verde, pass here.

Map continues on page 210

209

*One of many fine
viewpoints around
the village of
Artenara, above the
Barranco de Tejeda*

Rise and fall gently, keeping left at another path junction (Walk 16 heads right, for Altavista and La Aldea), down to a mirador, map-board, signpost and parking space at **Degollada del Sargento**, around 1160m (3805ft).

Turn right down the road to find a signpost on the right for Artenara and Cruz de Tejeda. The road makes a pronounced bend, while a path descends broad and even, becoming rocky as it re-joins the road. Go straight along the road and up through a crossroads. A path on the right zigzags uphill, on bare rock or with steps, past pines and a few tagasaste, lots of cistus and a few tabaibal. Climb steeply to a shoulder around 1300m (4265ft) on **Brezos**. Artenara can be seen ahead, with Moriscos beyond, as well as Pico de las Nieves and Roque Nublo.

Follow a track down to a mast and continue down to a junction of tracks and paths, signposts and map-boards. ◀ Follow the track ahead, with a helipad and cemetery to the left, and pines to the right, to join a road.

*Walk 14 heads
sharp right for
Vega de Acusa.*

210

Turn right down the road, reaching a main road and a roundabout on a gap. Walk straight up into the centre of **Artenara**, over 1200m (3940ft) (pensión, bar/restaurants, bank, post office and splendid viewpoints), where signposts indicate several destinations.

Cruz de Tejeda is signposted up the same road as La Cuevita at first, then climbs a concrete road. ▸ The road climbs steeply, then keep left and pause at a mirador on the left. The concrete road becomes a track, rising gently before heading down to a junction. Walk ahead to a map-board then up a stone-paved path for Cruz de Tejeda. Some stretches are cut into conglomerate bedrock. Keep right at a fork, up into pine forest. The path splits again, so keep left up a stone-paved path to a track.

Turn left up the track, but when it turns right, leave it and follow a path straight ahead, climbing to re-join the track at a higher point. Walk up it as signposted, climb straight ahead at a junction, reaching another track on a bend. Keep right and keep climbing, with a bit of a dip before climbing further. Continue up a path that winds and is often on bare rock overlooking Tejeda. Catch a glimpse of a bend on the track to the left at a higher level, and, as the ground steepens, the path drifts among pines and zigzags uphill without views. Level out later and re-join the track at a three-way signpost. Turn right up the track, then down to a gap. Note peculiar outcrops and huge boulders to the right, at a notice-board about **Cuevas Caballero**.

Consider detouring right to visit the Ermita Virgen de la Cuevita, where a chapel has been hewn from a thick bed of ash.

Map continues on page 213

Sunset near Cruz de Tejeda, with a view across the clouds to El Teide on Tenerife

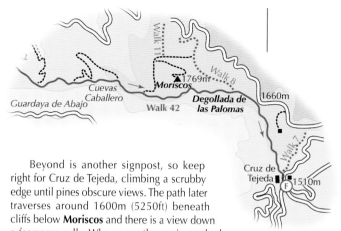

Beyond is another signpost, so keep right for Cruz de Tejeda, climbing a scrubby edge until pines obscure views. The path later traverses around 1600m (5250ft) beneath cliffs below **Moriscos** and there is a view down a fearsome gully. When a gentle gap is reached, the path heads left to join a track at a signpost. ▶ Turn right along the track and it becomes a well-worn path with steps down to a road, signposts and a viewpoint shelter at 1660m (5446ft) on **Degollada de las Palomas**.

Just beyond the shelter, go up a path on the right, which levels out to exploit a soft red layer. The slope is grazed by sheep and goats and enjoys views of Tejeda and Roque Nublo, with rugged pinnacles of rock nearby. The traverse gives way to a descent past pines, keeping right of a small stone-built reservoir. Drop steeply beside more pines to reach map-boards and a car park, around 1510m (4955ft). Turn right towards two hotels at **Cruz de Tejeda** – the Parador and the Hotel Rural El Refugio.

Left along the track is Walk 8, the PR GC 04 to Valleseco.

WALK 43
GR 131 – Cruz de Tejeda to San Bartolomé

Start	Cruz de Tejeda
Finish	San Bartolomé
Distance	15km (9½ miles)
Total Ascent	300m (985ft)
Total Descent	910m (2985ft)
Time	6hrs
Terrain	High-level paths, with occasional tracks and roads, often on forested slopes, occasionally steep and rugged for short stretches.
Refreshments	Bars at Cruz de Tejeda. Restaurant at Llanos de Garañón. Plenty of choice in San Bartolomé.
Transport	Occasional daily buses serve Cruz de Tejeda and San Bartolomé from San Mateo, Tejeda and Maspalomas.

The route south from Cruz de Tejeda stays high on a mountain crest, with gradients easing around Llanos de Garañón. Instead of climbing Pico de las Nieves, Gran Canaria's highest point, an old path with amazing engineering descends to Cruz Grande, linking with a path down to San Bartolomé.

Broad, stone-paved paths run parallel to the road on the way to Degollada Becerra

Leave **Cruz de Tejeda** (Walks 7 and 8 start here) by climbing beside El Refugio, signposted as the PR GC 40 for Llanos de la Pez. A short way above the hotel grounds is a path junction (Walk 25 descends to the right), so keep left and climb past bushes, emerging with fine views westwards. The path crosses the pine-forested slopes of **Morro de la Armonía**, linking with a track passing a building in a fenced enclosure around 1600m (5250ft). Leave the track on a bend and follow a gritty path across a slope of volcanic ash, going down a stone-paved ramp to a road.

Follow the road onwards, with a view down to Las Lagunetas and the **Barranco de la Mina**, entering a forest. The road emerges and a path climbs right, passes a building and is stone-paved as it runs parallel to the road. Step onto the road at **Degollada Becerra**, at 1548m (5079ft). ▶ There are views to Roque El Fraile, Roque Nublo, Roque Bentayga, Altavista, and distant El Teide on Tenerife. A path leads to a nearby visitor centre that might well be closed.

Climb steeply from the gap on a crest of broom and pine. The path later runs gently along the crest, parallel

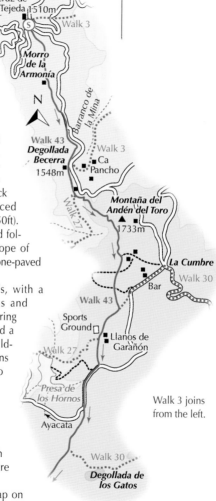

Walk 3 joins from the left.

Map continues on page 216

215

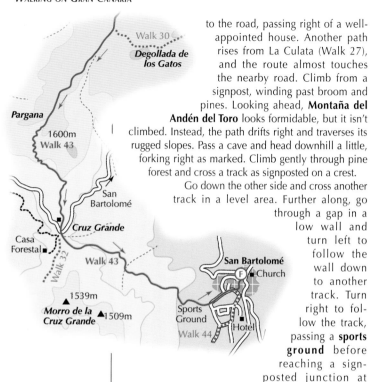

to the road, passing right of a well-appointed house. Another path rises from La Culata (Walk 27), and the route almost touches the nearby road. Climb from a signpost, winding past broom and pines. Looking ahead, **Montaña del Andén del Toro** looks formidable, but it isn't climbed. Instead, the path drifts right and traverses its rugged slopes. Pass a cave and head downhill a little, forking right as marked. Climb gently through pine forest and cross a track as signposted on a crest.

Go down the other side and cross another track in a level area. Further along, go through a gap in a low wall and turn left to follow the wall down to another track. Turn right to follow the track, passing a **sports ground** before reaching a signposted junction at **Llanos de Garañón**, around 1670m (5480ft). A large forest campsite and a restaurant lie to the left. ◄ Continue straight ahead down a broad, walled and fenced track, rising a short way, then go down to a road and signpost. Turn right to walk beside the road, first on the right, then on the left.

Walk 27 heads right.

A path on the left is signposted for Cruz Grande, as well as being the 'Camino de Santiago'. Follow the broad path, which is often worn to bedrock and has a low wall alongside, up a forested slope. Cross a streambed in a gentle dip, then follow a stone-paved path and steps, reaching bare rock. Look back to see Presa de los Hornos, with Moriscos far beyond. The path reaches a junction on a forested crest over 1700m (5580ft). ▶

Continue straight ahead and down a path that is stone-paved, or worn to earth and bedrock, among pines and broom. Emerge into a rocky area with a view down a barranco. Descend gently across the rock, avoiding a path heading up to the right. The path becomes clear and well-constructed across steep, rocky slopes, with a view down to San Bartolomé and the distant coast. Head in and out of pines and across bare rock, through a shallow valley at **Pargana**, around 1600m (5250ft), where a strip of vegetation follows a small stream.

Walk straight down a splendid stone-paved path, then zigzag round bushy corners, passing a stand of pines on largely rocky slopes. Views are splendid and a small reservoir is perched on a shelf to the right. There are cliffs, sometimes overhanging, but the path exploits rocky breaches and has impressive buttresses. A level traverse runs beneath a cliff, passing almond trees and bushy scrub. A rough and rocky ridge falls with scrubby slopes, and the path goes on top of it a couple of times.

Walk 30 turns left for Pico de las Nieves.

Bare rock on a forested slope, with a view back towards Moriscos

The Riscos de San Bartolomé tower above the town of San Bartolomé

To omit San Bartolomé, go through the cutting and follow Walk 32 to Degollada de la Manzanilla.

San Bartolomé is in view as a rugged stone-paved path descends to a house. A stone-paved track drops to **Cruz Grande**, where a right turn follows a road towards a rock cutting, around 1250m (4100ft). ◀

To descend to San Bartolomé, don't go through the cutting, but turn left as signposted for the PR GC 40, down a track. Turn left and right and follow a path with winding descents with fine views. Gentler rising and falling traverses are followed by a steep zigzag descent on the rocky, forested slope. Wind down a stone-paved path with steps, continuing down a track into a flat area with a sports ground nearby.

Turn left along Calle Juglar Fabian Torres, and right along Calle Manuel Zenón Araño Yánez. Turn left along and down Calle El Roque, and right down Calle San Juan, turning left and right. Turn left along Calle del Corazón de Jesús, and right down the brick-paved Calle Padre Claret. Turn left at the bottom to finish at the church in **San Bartolomé**, around 900m (2950ft) (hotel, pensión, banks with ATMs, post office, shops, bars, restaurants, buses and taxis).

WALK 44

GR 131 – San Bartolomé to Ayagaures

Start	San Bartolomé
Finish	Ayagaures
Distance	16km (10 miles)
Total Ascent	375m (1230ft)
Total Descent	675m (2215ft)
Time	5hrs
Terrain	Apart from steep and rugged paths on the first ascent, and a descent on a forested slope, a dirt road undulates easily through a long barranco.
Refreshments	Plenty of choice in San Bartolomé. Bar at Ayagaures.
Transport	Occasional daily buses serve San Bartolomé from San Mateo, Tejeda and Maspalomas. Taxi required from Ayagaures.

Cultivated countryside around San Bartolomé quickly gives way to rugged slopes, with an old mule path climbing over Degollada de la Manzanilla. A forested descent leads to remote farms, where a long dirt road leads through the Barranco de la Data to the nearest village – Ayagaures.

Start at the church in the middle of **San Bartolomé**, around 900m (2950ft) (hotel, pensión, banks with ATMs, post office, shops, bars, restaurants, buses and taxis). Walk into the village and turn right up the brick-paved Calle Padre Claret. Turn left up the tarmac Calle del Corazón de Jesús. Turn right up Calle San Juan, which turns left and right with a view of the village and mountains. Turn left up Calle El Roque, which levels out to reach a junction. Continue along Avenida Teniente Alcalde Antonio Santana. There are turnings left for the **Hotel Las Tirajanas** and right for a **sports ground**, but keep straight ahead.

Turn right along a minor road signposted as the PR GC 40 to Degollada de la Manzanilla. Turn left at a junction and follow a road rising gently. Take the second farm track on the right, as signposted, which becomes steeper and concrete up to a farm at **Llano Pelado**. Turn right, not up among pines, but down a little past a fenced field. The track rises and is flanked by bushy scrub, then the gradient eases. Scree is crossed and rock-fall debris means the track can not be used by vehicles. When the broad path turns right round a corner there are tottering pinnacles of rock above.

Continue along the base of a cliff where the path exploits a soft, creamy layer of rock, sometimes beneath big overhangs. Climb a winding, stone-paved or stone-strewn path, held in place by massive stone buttresses. The scrub includes calcosas, tajinaste, tabaibal, broom, aloes and lavender, with a few pines dotted around. Reach a three-way signpost at a junction with a forest track on **Degollada de la Manzanilla**. Looking across the gap, an expanse of dry pine forest covers every slope and summit. ◄

Walk 32 joins from the right.

A narrow path at the base of a cliff between San Bartolomé and Degollada de la Manzanilla

La Cruz de Umbria, where funeral processions paused on a rugged slope

Turn left and follow the track signposted for Maspalomas, rising and falling gently, with cliffs above. Turn right as signposted down a stone-paved path, squeezing through calcosas. A stony path zigzags down a slope covered in pines, becoming worn and stony. Avoid other paths to right and left, cross a forest track and continue down, then

Map continues on page 222

221

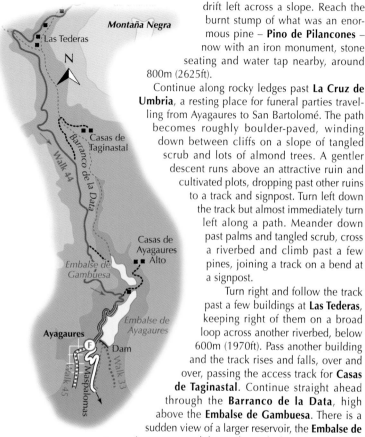

Montaña Negra

Las Tederas

N

Casas de
Taginastal

Walk 44

Barranco de la Data

Casas de
Ayagaures
Alto

Embalse de
Gambuesa

Ayagaures

Embalse de
Ayagaures

Dam

Walk 45

Maspalomas

Walk 33

Walk 33 crosses
the dam.

drift left across a slope. Reach the burnt stump of what was an enormous pine – **Pino de Pilancones** – now with an iron monument, stone seating and water tap nearby, around 800m (2625ft).

Continue along rocky ledges past **La Cruz de Umbria**, a resting place for funeral parties travelling from Ayagaures to San Bartolomé. The path becomes roughly boulder-paved, winding down between cliffs on a slope of tangled scrub and lots of almond trees. A gentler descent runs above an attractive ruin and cultivated plots, dropping past other ruins to a track and signpost. Turn left down the track but almost immediately turn left along a path. Meander down past palms and tangled scrub, cross a riverbed and climb past a few pines, joining a track on a bend at a signpost.

Turn right and follow the track past a few buildings at **Las Tederas**, keeping right of them on a broad loop across another riverbed, below 600m (1970ft). Pass another building and the track rises and falls, over and over, passing the access track for **Casas de Taginastal**. Continue straight ahead through the **Barranco de la Data**, high above the **Embalse de Gambuesa**. There is a sudden view of a larger reservoir, the **Embalse de Ayagaures**, and the track winds down towards it. A road rises and falls alongside, leading towards the dam and a signpost. ◄ Keep right to enter the little village of **Ayagaures**, around 300m (985ft), where there is a bar. There are no buses from here, but a taxi can be called from Maspalomas. Alternatively, continue along Walk 45 for 12km (7½ miles) to Aqualand to catch a bus.

WALK 45
GR 131 – Ayagaures to Faro de Maspalomas

Start	Ayagaures
Finish	Faro de Maspalomas
Distance	18km (11 miles)
Total Ascent	250m (820ft)
Total Descent	550m (1805ft)
Time	5hrs
Terrain	Entirely along roads, starting with a steep climb and a later descent, then running level all the way through Maspalomas to the coast.
Refreshments	Bars at Ayagaures, Caserio La Montaña and near Aqualand. Plenty of choice in Maspalomas.
Transport	Taxi required to Ayagaures. Regular daily buses link Aqualand and Maspalomas.

This final stage of the trek through Gran Canaria is entirely along or beside roads. The first part involves a zigzag road to a gap, followed by a mountain road to a village. The descent onto flat ground leads to the built-up resort of Maspalomas, and the end of the long trail is at a landmark lighthouse.

Leave **Ayagaures**, around 300m (985ft), by walking uphill from the chapel, plaza and bar. The road rises and falls as it leaves the village, then a relentless series of bends and zigzags climb a steep, scrub-covered slope, notable for the tall, yellow umbellifers called cañalejas. Towards the top of the slope, the road slices across a cliff to reach a gap, passing a signpost for the PR GC 40. There is a house nearby, and a fine view across the Barranco de la Data from **Cima Pedro González** at 490m (1608ft).

Follow the mountain road onwards, overlooking **Palmitos Park**, which is usually busy with visitors. ▶ Pass a house, Cumbre del Sol, and stay on the road, avoiding other roads to left and right. Wind down below houses at

There is no way down to Palmitos Park from this road.

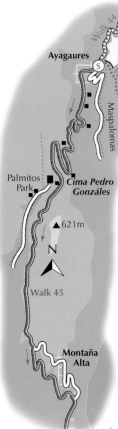

Montaña Alta and the road becomes flanked by palm trees and pavements. Keep right at a roundabout, down a palm-fringed road, then uphill without palms alongside. A crest is reached and there is a view down to the coast, taking in Playa del Inglés and Maspalomas, with the Dunas de Maspalomas in-between.

There are cliffs on both sides of the road, which then runs through a village, **Caserio La Montaña**. On the way downhill, pass a shop

View of the Barranco de la Data and Ayagaures from Cima Pedro González

and bar/restaurants, around 200m (655ft). The road overlooks a camel park before dropping to a junction. Turn left along a busy road, passing **Aqualand**, where buses stop. Use a stony path alongside the road to pass the **Karting** attraction, which has a bar/restaurant. Follow the road onwards, passing beneath a busy main road supported by concrete pillars.

Go through a roundabout as signposted for Maspalomas, and use a footpath and cycleway to the right of the road. Stay on this side to pass a huge roundabout at **Sonnenland**. Get onto the top deck of the Sonnenland Centre and use a footbridge to cross over the main road. This allows a splendid footpath and cycleway to be used, winding through a linear plantation of palm trees to the left of the main road. Cross a riverbed while passing another roundabout on the way into Maspalomas (a major resort with a full range of facilities), now without shade, probably in the hottest part of the day.

Either follow the pavement straight ahead beside the road, or use a bendy green cycleway a little further away, passing another roundabout. The next roundabout is quite distinctive

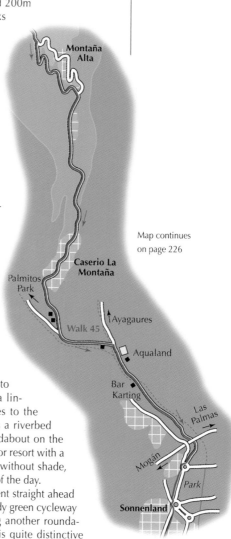

Map continues
on page 226

225

A palm-shaded path can be followed away from Sonnenland towards Maspalomas

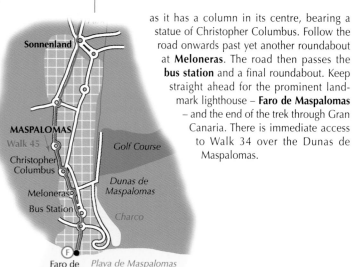

as it has a column in its centre, bearing a statue of Christopher Columbus. Follow the road onwards past yet another roundabout at **Meloneras**. The road then passes the **bus station** and a final roundabout. Keep straight ahead for the prominent landmark lighthouse – **Faro de Maspalomas** – and the end of the trek through Gran Canaria. There is immediate access to Walk 34 over the Dunas de Maspalomas.

APPENDIX A

Route summary table

Walk	Start	Finish	Distance	Total Ascent	Total Descent	Time	Page
1	Vegueta, Las Palmas	Santa Brígida	16km (10 miles)	550m (1805ft)	50m (165ft)	5hrs	36
2	Las Meleguinas	Las Lagunetas	14km (8½ miles)	850m (2790ft)	50m (165ft)	5hrs	41
3	Las Lagunetas	Las Lagunetas	8km (5 miles)	550m (1805ft)	550m (1805ft)	3hrs	45
4	Santa Brígida	Teror	12km (7½ miles)	550m (1805ft)	450m (1475ft)	4hrs	49
5	San Mateo	Teror	11km (7 miles)	450m (1475ft)	675m (2215ft)	4 hrs	52
6	Casas de la Caldera, Bandama	Casas de la Caldera, Bandama	8km (5 miles)	275m (900ft)	275m (900ft)	3hrs	57
7	Cruz de Tejeda	Teror	12km (7½ miles)	200m (655ft)	1120m (3675ft)	3hrs 30mins	61
8	Cruz de Tejeda	Valleseco	12km (7½ miles)	510m (1675ft)	1070m (3510ft)	4hrs	66
9	Cruz de La Laguna	Cruz de La Laguna	12km (7½ miles)	600m (1970ft)	600m (1970ft)	4hrs	70
10	Cruz de La Laguna	Cruz de La Laguna	13km (8 miles)	500m (1640ft)	500m (1640ft)	4hrs 30mins	75
11	Between Montañón Negro and Moriscos	Santa María de Guía	22km (13¾ miles)	250m (820ft)	1830m (6005ft)	7hrs	81
12	Artenara	Campsite, Tamadaba	13km (8 miles)	500m (1640ft)	540m (1770ft)	4hrs	86
13	San Pedro	San Pedro	16km (10 miles)	1200m (3940ft)	1200m (3940ft)	5hrs 30mins	91
14	Acusa Seca	Acusa Seca	7km (4½ miles)	250m (820ft)	250m (820ft)	2hrs 30mins	95

227

Walk	Start	Finish	Distance	Total Ascent	Total Descent	Time	Page
15	Casa Forestal de Tirma	Andén Verde	19km (12 miles)	150m (490ft)	800m (2625ft)	5hrs	100
16	Degollada del Sargento	La Aldea	20km (12½ miles)	470m (1540ft)	1570m (5150ft)	7hrs	103
17	La Aldea	El Risco	15km (9½ miles)	800m (2625ft)	800m (2625ft)	5hrs	108
18	Albercón	Tasártico	15km (9½ miles)	1400m (4595ft)	1250m (4100ft)	6hrs	112
19	Degollada de La Aldea	La Aldea	12km (7½ miles)	400m (1310ft)	1000m (3280ft)	5hrs	117
20	El Aserrador	Casas de la Umbría	15km (9½ miles)	950m (3115ft)	1260m (4135ft)	5hrs	122
21	El Aserrador	El Aserrador	13km (8 miles)	710m (2330ft)	710m (2330ft)	4hrs	127
22	Cruce de la Data	Cruce de la Data	10km (6¼ miles)	305m (1000ft)	305m (1000ft)	3hrs	129
23	Cruce de San Antonio	Las Casillas, Mógan	13km (8 miles)	380m (1245ft)	1150m (3775ft)	4hrs	131
24	Paso Herradura	Cruce de la Data	15km (9½ miles)	485m (1590ft)	760m (2495ft)	5hrs	136
25	Tejeda	Tejeda	7km (4½ miles)	100m (1640ft)	500m (1640ft)	2hrs 30mins	142
26	Tejeda	Tejeda	9km (5½ miles)	500m (1640ft)	500m (1640ft)	3hrs	145
27	Degollada Becerra	Degollada Becerra	9km (5½ miles)	650m (2130ft)	650m (2130ft)	3hrs	148
28	La Goleta, above Ayacata	La Goleta, above Ayacata	5km (3 miles)	350m (1150ft)	350m (1150ft)	2hrs	152
29	Cruz Grande	Ayacata	9km (5½ miles)	460m (1510ft)	410m (1345ft)	3hrs	154
30	Llanos de Garañón	Llanos de Garañón	11km (7 miles)	350m (1150ft)	350m (1150ft)	3hrs 30mins	158

Walk	Start	Finish	Distance	Total Ascent	Total Descent	Time	Page
31	Santa Lucía	Cruz Grande	20km (12½ miles)	1450m (4760ft)	880m (2890ft)	8hrs	162
32	San Bartolomé	San Bartolomé	14km (8¾ miles)	400m (1310ft)	400m (1310ft)	4hrs	167
33	Arteara	Ayagaures	15km (9½ miles)	175m (575ft)	225m (740ft)	5hrs	171
34	Faro de Maspalomas	Faro de Maspalomas	6km (3¾ miles)	30m (100ft)	30m (100ft)	2hrs	174
35	Siete Fuentes	San Mateo	8km (5 miles)	1060m (3480ft)	55m (180ft)	2hrs 30mins	178
36	San Mateo	Valsequillo	8km (5 miles)	250m (820ft)	525m (1720ft)	3hrs	181
37	Valsequillo	Santa Brígida	9km (5½ miles)	450m (1475ft)	500m (1640ft)	3hrs	185
38	El Rincón	El Rincón	8km (5 miles)	1250m (4100ft)	1250m (4100ft)	4hrs	189
39	Tenteniguada	Valsequillo	12km (7½ miles)	800m (2625ft)	800m (2625ft)	5hrs	193
40	Caldera de los Marteles	Valsequillo	12km (7½ miles)	150m (490ft)	1150m (3775ft)	4hrs	199
41	Puerto de las Nieves	Campsite, Tamadaba	12km (7½ miles)	1250m (4100ft)	50m (165ft)	4hrs	204
42	Campsite, Tamadaba	Cruz de Tejeda	17km (10½ miles)	1000m (3280ft)	670m (2200ft)	6hrs	208
43	Cruz de Tejeda	San Bartolomé	15km (9½ miles)	300m (985ft)	910m (2985ft)	6hrs	214
44	San Bartolomé	Ayagaures	16km (10 miles)	375m (1230ft)	675m (2215ft)	5hrs	219
45	Ayagaures	Faro de Maspalomas	18km (11 miles)	250m (820ft)	550m (1805ft)	5hrs	223

APPENDIX B
Topographical glossary

Apart from a few place-names derived from original Guanche words, most names appearing on maps are Spanish. Many words appear frequently and are usually descriptive of landforms or colours. The following list of common words helps to sort out what some of the places on maps or signposts mean.

Spanish	English
Agua	Water
Alto/Alta	High
Arenas	Sands
Arroyo	Stream
Asomada	Promontory
Bajo/Baja	Low
Barranco	Ravine
Barranquillo	Small Ravine
Blanco/Blanca	White
Boca	Gap
Cabeza	Head
Caldera	Crater
Calle	Street
Camino	Path/Track
Cañada	Gully
Canal	Watercourse
Carretera	Road
Casa	House
Casa Forestal	Forestry House
Caseta	Small House/Hut
Collada/Degollada	Col/Gap/Saddle

Spanish	English
Colorada	Coloured
Cruz	Cross/Crossroads
Cueva	Cave
Cumbre	Ridge/Crest
De/Del	Of the
El/La/Los/Las	The
Embalse	Reservoir
Era	Threshing Floor
Ermita	Chapel/Shrine
Estacion de Guaguas	Bus Station
Fuente	Fountain/Spring
Gordo	Fat/Giant
Grande	Big
Guagua	Bus
Hoya	Valley
Ladera	Slope
Llano	Plain
Lomo	Spur/Ridge
Mirador	Viewpoint
Montaña	Mountain

Looking up at the Barranco del Juncal, from El Juncal to El Aserrador (Walk 21)

Spanish	English
Morro	Nose
Negro/Negra	Black
Nieve	Snow
Nuevo/Nueva	New
Parada	Bus Stop
Paso	Pass
Pequeño	Small
Pico	Peak
Piedra	Rock
Pino/Pinar	Pine
Playa	Beach
Plaza	Town Square
Presa	Small Reservoir
Puerto	Port
Punta	Point

Spanish	English
Risco	Cliff
Roja	Red
Roque	Rock
San/Santa	Saint (male/female)
Sendero	Route/Path
Valle	Valley
Verde	Green
Vieja/Viejo	Old
Volcán	Volcano

APPENDIX C
Useful contacts

Travel and transport

Inter-island flights
Binter Canarias,
tel 902-381110 or 928-252630,
www.bintercanarias.com

Inter-island ferries
Lineas Fred Olsen,
tel 902-100107,
www.fredolsen.es

Naviera Armas, tel 902-456500,
www.naviera-armas.com

Bus services
Global, tel 922-531300,
www.globalsu.es

Canary Islands tourism
General Canary Islands tourism,
www.turismodecanarias.com

Canary Islands eco-tourism,
www.ecoturismocanarias.com

Gran Canaria tourism,
www.grancanaria.com

Tourist information offices
Las Palmas – There are several offices
and information points around the
city, but the main one is on Calle
Triana, tel 928-219600.

Maspalomas/Playa del Inglés –
There are several offices and
information points around the resorts,
but the main one is at Yumbo,
tel 928 771 550.

Airport, tel 928-574117
Agüimes, tel 928-124183
Artenara, tel 928-666102
Arucas, tel 928-623136
Firgas, tel 928-616747
Gáldar, tel 928-895855
Ingenio, tel 928-783799
La Aldea (San Nicolás),
tel 928-890378
Mógan, 928-158804
Moya, tel 928-612348
Puerto de las Nieves, tel 928-554382
San Agustín, tel 928-769262
San Mateo, tel 928-661350
Santa Brígida, tel 928-648181
Santa Lucía, tel 928-125260
Santa María de Guía, tel 928-553043
Tejeda, tel 928-666189
Telde, tel 928-013312
Teror, tel 928-613808
Valleseco, tel 928-618740
Valsequillo, tel 928-705011

Wild camping is illegal, but it happens. There are small, basic campsites around the island

Island Government (Cabildo)

Cabildo de Gran Canaria,
http://portal.grancanaria.com

Camping permits

There are 20 basic state-run campsites dotted around Gran Canaria, which are available free of charge, provided a permit is obtained in advance. Permits can be applied for in English on the Cabildo de Gran Canaria website, clicking on the word 'Acampadas'.

Please read the English version of the rules and regulations. Next, find the words 'formulario web' and click on the English version to find the application form for permits. Note that permits must be collected in person, and anyone found using one of the campsites without a permit risks being evicted. Wild camping is technically illegal, but also surprisingly popular.

NOTES

NOTES

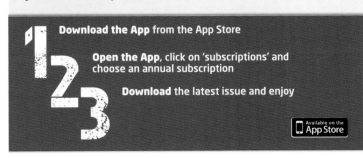

LISTING OF CICERONE GUIDES

For full information on all our
guides, and to order books and
eBooks, visit our website:
www.cicerone.co.uk.

Walking – Trekking – Mountaineering – Climbing – Cycling

Over 40 years, Cicerone have built up an outstanding collection of 300 guides, inspiring all sorts of amazing adventures.

Every guide comes from extensive exploration and research by our expert authors, all with a passion for their subjects. They are frequently praised, endorsed and used by clubs, instructors and outdoor organisations.

All our titles can now be bought as **e-books** and many as iPad and Kindle files and we will continue to make all our guides available for these and many other devices.

Our website shows any **new information** we've received since a book was published. Please do let us know if you find anything has changed, so that we can pass on the latest details. On our **website** you'll also find some great ideas and lots of information, including sample chapters, contents lists, reviews, articles and a photo gallery.

It's easy to keep in touch with what's going on at Cicerone, by getting our monthly **free e-newsletter**, which is full of offers, competitions, up-to-date information and topical articles. You can subscribe on our home page and also follow us on **Facebook** and **Twitter**, as well as our **blog**.

Cicerone – the very best guides for exploring the world.

CICERONE

2 Police Square Milnthorpe Cumbria LA7 7PY
Tel: 015395 62069 info@cicerone.co.uk
www.cicerone.co.uk